SELECTED POEMS AND PROSE

Guittone d'Arezzo

THE LORENZO DA PONTE ITALIAN LIBRARY

THE DA PONTE ITALIAN LIBRARY

Guittone d'Arezzo

SELECTED POEMS AND PROSE

Selected, Translated, and with an Introduction by Antonello Borra

UNIVERSITY OF TORONTO PRESS
Toronto Buffalo London

Toronto Buffalo London
www.utppublishing.com

ISBN 978-1-4875-0124-2

The Lorenzo Da Ponte Italian Library

Library and Archives Canada Cataloguing in Publication

Guittone, d'Arezzo, –1294
[Works. Selections]
Selected poems and prose / Guittone d'Arezzo ; selected, translated, and with an introduction by Antonello Borra.

(The Lorenzo Da Ponte Italian library)
Includes bibliographical references and index.
Text in Italian with English translation on facing pages.
ISBN 978-1-4875-0124-2 (cloth)

1. Guittone, d'Arezzo, –1294 – Translations into English. I. Borra, Antonello, 1963–, translator, editor II. Guittone, d'Arezzo, –1294. Works. Selections. English. III. Title IV. Series: Lorenzo Da Ponte Italian library

PQ4472.G7A2 2017 851'.1 C2016-908193-1

University of Toronto Press acknowledges the financial assistance to its publishing program of the Canada Council for the Arts and the Ontario Arts Council, an agency of the Government of Ontario.

Canada Council for the Arts Conseil des Arts du Canada

Funded by the Government of Canada Financé par le gouvernement du Canada | Canada

Contents

Acknowledgments

More than ten years of work went into the preparation of this book, and there are many people to whom I am greatly indebted. First and foremost, my friend and colleague Anis Memon, without whose constant help throughout the years this book would never have been completed. I owe him much more than this short note can express. I also wish to acknowledge my wife, Adriana Hoesle Borra, for her daily support; Francesca Geymonat, for many consultations; Zyg Baransky, Ted Cachey, Christian Moevs, and Stephen Little for their encouragement; Lino Pertile, who originally steered me towards Guittone; and Tony Oldcorn, my mentor at Brown. I would also like to acknowledge all the anonymous reviewers who, at different stages, supplied very precious feedback and advice and allowed me to amend many flaws and improve the quality of my work. My gratitude also goes to Gino Ruozzi, Paola Vecchi, and the Commissione per i Testi di Lingua di Bologna, to the Istituto della Enciclopedia Italiana, and to Casalini Libri for their kind permissions to reprint Guittone's original texts in reliable critical editions. I also wish to acknowledge Taylor and Francis LLC Books for their kind permission to reproduce parts of an article of mine originally published in *Encyclopedia of Italian Literary Studies*, ed. G. Marrone (New York and London: Routledge, 2007). Finally, I would like to remember the late Michelangelo Picone who several years ago accepted my first work on Guittone for the series he directed for Angelo Longo Editore.

I am also very thankful to the Office of the Vice President for Research, the College of Arts and Sciences, the Humanities Center, and the Department of Romance Languages and Linguistics at the University of Vermont for their generous support.

Preface

Guittone d'Arezzo was the most successful, innovative, influential, and prolific poet of his generation. Yet his fame did not much outlast the poet's death, and for centuries since, his literary greatness has been called into question. To redress this wrong would involve pointing out the individual responsible for a thorough, systematic, and ultimately unjust *damnatio memoriae* that has succeeded beyond any reasonable expectation. This poses a not negligible difficulty, however, as the individual in question is none other than Dante Alighieri, whose works form the basis of the Italian literary canon and marginalize poor Guittone. Yet in order to understand the cultural and artistic value of Guittone's work as a whole, it does not help matters to simply reverse Dante's judgments; nor does it help to pretend that his judgments do not continue in one way or another to influence that value when we examine it in context. Guittone's lyric emerged against the backdrop of the Occitan and Oïl language traditions, the poetry of the troubadours, the trouvères, and the *Roman de la rose*.[1] It was in direct competition with the very recent experiences of the poets of Emperor Frederick II's itinerant court (the so-called Sicilian School),[2] and alongside the experiments of the Tuscan poets of the day,

1 A good introduction and an excellent bilingual selection of troubadour texts in English is the one provided by Frede Jensen in *Troubadour Lyrics*. For a selection including texts by both troubadours and trouvères, see Frederick Goldin, *Lyrics of the Troubadours and Trouvères*; for the *Rose* see Frances Horgan's translation and annotated edition: *The Romance of the Rose*.

2 For an introduction and a bilingual selection of texts in English, see Frede Jensen's *The Poetry of the Sicilian School*.

many of whom corresponded with Guittone and were retroactively labelled "Guittonians."[3]

There is no doubt that critical research of the last twenty years – beginning at least with the Arezzo conference of 1994 commemorating the 700th anniversary of the poet's death[4] – has done wonders to render unto Guittone the things that are Guittone's. And the ideas presented here, in both my introduction and the explanatory notes to the texts, are largely a compendium of that research. But the main impetus for this work is to provide English-speaking readers – teachers or students, passionate admirers of poetry and medieval literature or the merely curious – with something that has hitherto been unavailable, namely a representative and relatively substantial anthology of the works of Guittone d'Arezzo, a poet whose importance, Petrarch seems to imply,[5] surpassed even that of the more commonly applauded Guido Guinizzelli and Ezra Pound's hero, Guido Cavalcanti.[6]

3 For an introduction and a bilingual selection of texts in English, see Frede Jensen's *Tuscan Poetry of the Duecento.*

4 The conference proceedings were published in Picone, ed., *Guittone d'Arezzo nel settimo centenario della morte.*

5 See Petrarch's *Triumphus Cupidinis*: "[...] ecco Dante e Beatrice, ecco Selvaggia, / ecco Cin da Pistoia, Guitton d'Arezzo, / che di non esser primo par ch'ir aggia; / ecco i due Guidi, che già furo in prezzo, / Onesto Bolognese, e i ciciliani, / che già fur primi e quivi eran da sezzo" [Here is Dante and Beatrice, here is Selvaggia, here is Cino da Pistoia, Guittone d'Arezzo, who seems angry not to be the first, here are the two Guidos, who were praiseworthy, Onesto Bolognese and the Sicilians, who used to be first and now merely follow] (*Triumphus Cupidinis* iv, 31–6; my translation); Ariani, ed., *Triumphi.*

6 For Guinizzelli's texts in English, see Robert Edwards's edition, *The Poetry of Guido Guinizzelli.* For Cavalcanti's texts in English, see Lowry Nelson, Jr's edition, *The Poetry of Guido Cavalcanti,* as well as the more recent selection by Simon West, *The Selected Poetry of Guido Cavalcanti.*

SELECTED POEMS AND PROSE

Guittone d'Arezzo

Introduction

The Great Enemy

If we set aside the Provençal-influenced court poets of the Sicilian School, Guittone's place in Italian literary history coincides with that history's very beginnings, from which Dante, in his programmatic discussion of the ideal literary language, *De vulgari eloquentia*, was the first to suggest, or rather *insist*, that Guittone be marginalized. Dante does not merely attack his predecessor directly, but in choosing examples of excellence in versification, both for the hendecasyllabic line and the *canzone*, he bypasses him entirely. In his treatise, Dante traces Italy's poetic genealogy directly back to the Occitan and Oïl language models that the chief poets of the Sicilian School – Giacomo da Lentini in particular – and the poets of the next generation, like Guido Guinizzelli, Guido Cavalcanti, Cino da Pistoia, and, naturally, Dante himself, had followed.

Whether we admit it or not, Dante's biased judgment very often still guides our basic notions about Guittone; it is therefore important to get a sense of the breadth and weight of his condemnation. In order to see how systematic Dante's attacks were, we have only to recall that Guittone's name appears explicitly in two strategic locations in *De vulgari eloquentia* and the *Comedy*. Furthermore, the *Vita nova* contains weighty and explicit attacks on intellectuals who cannot be precisely identified but in whom a moment's reflection cannot fail to discern the figure of Guittone.

In both books of *De vulgari eloquentia*, Dante directly singles out Guittone. In chapter XIII of the first book, he uses him as an example of those Tuscan authors who continue to express themselves largely in parochial language, deluding themselves that their vocabulary is suited to poetic diction, or rather to that prestigious vernacular, the so-called *volgare illustre,* whose precise characteristics Dante's uncompleted Latin treatise was trying to define.[1]

The second attack can be found in chapter VI of the second book, and this time concerns the use of vulgar words and constructions.[2]

It is clear that Dante considered the language of Guittone's lyric plebeian and not literary, vulgar and not aristocratically elevated, as is necessary for true poetry; therefore, those who glorify Guittone and his followers must be ignorant. This is the judgment that the exiled Dante pronounced, around 1307, on the most important and influential poet of the preceding generation – from whom he himself had learned a great deal.[3]

And Dante did not tone down his criticism in his own masterpiece. There are two additional places in the *Comedy* in which he excoriates the poet from Arezzo, both of these in *Purgatory.*

In canto XXIV, Bonagiunta da Lucca, considered by many to be a follower of Guittone, listens to the Pilgrim's claim that his writings are divinely inspired and admits to the inferiority of his own poetry.[4]

---

1 "Post hec veniamus ad Tuscos, qui propter amentiam suam infroniti titulum sibi vulgaris illustris arrogare videntur. Et in hoc non solum plebeia dementat intentio, sed famosos quamplures viros hoc tenuisse comperimus: puta Guittonem Aretinum, qui nunquam se ad curiale vulgare direxit ..." (I, xiii, 1) [After this, we come to the Tuscans, who, rendered senseless by some aberration of their own, seem to lay claim to the honor of possessing the illustrious vernacular. And it is not only the common people who lose their heads in this fashion, for we find that a number of famous men have believed as much: like Guittone d'Arezzo, who never even aimed at a vernacular worthy of the court ...]. English translations for both passages are taken from Steven Botterill's edition. The most recent edition of Dante's text is the one offered by *Opere: Rime. Vita nova. De vulgari eloquentia,* ed. M. Santagata.

2 "Subsistant igitur ignorantie sectatores Guictonem Aretinum et quosdam alios extollentes, nunquam in vocabulis atque constructione plebescere desuetos" (II, vi, 8) [So let the devotees of ignorance cease to cry up Guittone d'Arezzo and others like him, for never, in either vocabulary or construction, have they been anything but commonplace].

3 For a summary of Dante's debts and his overall relation to Guittone, see at least Gorni, "Guittone e Dante"; Antonelli, "Subsistant igitur ignorantie sectatores"; and Mazzoni, "Tematiche politiche tra Guittone e Dante," in Picone's edited volume *Guittone d'Arezzo nel settimo centenario della morte: Atti del convegno internazionale di Arezzo.*

4 "'O frate, issa vegg'io,' diss'elli, 'il nodo / che il Notaro e Guittone e me ritenne / di qua dal dolce stil novo ch'i' odo! / Io veggio ben come le vostre penne / di retro al dittator sen vanno strette, / che de le nostre certo non avvenne; / e qual più a gradire oltre si mette, / non vede più da l'uno a l'altro stilo'" (*Purg.* XXIV, 55–62) ["O my brother, now I see," said he, "the knot that held the Notary and Guittone and me back on this side of the sweet new style I hear. I see well how your pens follow close behind him who dictates, which with ours certainly did not happen; and whoever most sets himself to looking further will not see any other difference between the

This, apparently, is the true differentiator between the poetry of the Sicilian and Guittonian schools on the one hand and that of Dante on the other. The difference is one of substance and not of style; the limitation that held back Guittone and the poets whom Bonagiunta admired and imitated lies in their inability to follow Love's true dictates.[5] Later on, in *Purgatory* XXVI, Dante's censure is even clearer, though also more subtle. Here the speaker is none other than Guido Guinizzelli, whom the Pilgrim has just called his poetic "father," a term that Guinizzelli had once used in a sonnet to refer, perhaps ironically, to Guittone.[6] The poet from Bologna claims that Guittone's supremacy among the readers of the previous century was as unjustified as that accorded by many, including Dante himself,[7] to Giraut de Bornelh.[8] The troubadour from Périgord (rather than from Limoges), who sings of the moral righteousness considered superior to love poetry in *De vulgari eloquentia*, must now step aside and give the floor to the poet who speaks after Guinizzelli – Arnaut Daniel, the *miglior fabbro del parlar materno* (better artisan of the mother tongue; 117). One thing is quite clear from the complex redefinition of poetic genealogies that Dante attempts in this part of *Purgatory*: only fools who give their own opinion without having adequate artistic and intellectual qualifications can still admire Guittone.

To get a complete picture of Dante's attitude towards Guittone in the *Comedy*, it is not enough simply to look at the places where the latter's name appears. More than one critic has noted that Oderisi's discourse on the vanity of earthly fame in canto XI of *Purgatory* could very well

---

one style and the other"]. The English text of the *Commedia* here (and later) is given in Robert M. Durling's translation. Here, it is *Purgatorio*, ed. Durling and Martinez

5 On the complex issue of the "knot," see at least Gorni, "Il nodo della lingua"; Pertile, "Il nodo di Bonagiunta, le penne di Dante e il Dolce Stil Novo"; and Baranski, "'’nfiata labbia' and 'dolce stil novo.'"

6 On Guinizzelli's text and its interpretations, see Borsa, "La tenzone con Guittone d'Arezzo." Also Justin Steinberg agrees on the the parodic sense of the sonnet; see *Accounting for Dante*, 36–9. For a more recent contribution, see Rea, "Guinizzelli 'praised and explained.'"

7 See *De vulgari eloquentia*, II, ii, 9.

8 "e lascia dir gli stolti / che quel di Lemosì credon ch'avanzi. / A voce più che al ver drizzan li volti, / e così ferman sua oppinione / prima ch'arte o ragion per lor s'ascolti. / Così fer molti antichi di Guittone, / di grido in grido pur lui dando pregio, / fin che l'ha vinto il ver con più persone" (*Purg.* XXVI, 119–26) [no matter what the fools say who think that the one from near Limoges is better. They turn their faces more to reputation than to the truth, and thus they fix their opinion before listening to art or reason. Thus of old many did with Guittone, still praising him in cry after cry, until the truth overcame him in the judgment of more people].

allude to Guittone.[9] If, as is probable, the name "Guittone" is a modification of "Guido," then it makes sense that one of the two poets mentioned in this passage is in fact the one we are interested in.[10]

But there is more, and this time we find ourselves in canto XXIII of the *Inferno,* which contains the sixth pouch of the eighth Circle where hypocrites march slowly beneath leaden cloaks. The two damned figures that the Pilgrim meets, and upon whose sins he ironically refuses to comment when he interrupts the sentence, are none other than the founders of the religious order of the *Milites Beatae Virginis Mariae* (Knights of the Blessed Virgin Mary), commonly referred to as the Jovial Friars, to which Guittone belonged and for whom he was the intellectual spokesperson.[11] And much to the Pilgrim's surprise, he meets another Jovial Friar, brother Alberigo, in canto XXXIII, among the traitors. At the time of Dante's otherworldly journey, Alberigo was still living, but his soul had already been condemned for eternity.[12] It is clear that even though Guittone's name is not mentioned in the *Inferno,* a reader who knows that he was a

9 "Credette Cimabue ne la pittura / tener lo campo, e ora ha Giotto il grido, / sì che la fama di colui è scura: / così ha tolto l'uno a l'altro Guido / la gloria de la lingua; e forse è nato / chi l'uno e l'altro caccerà del nido" (*Purg.* XI, 94–9) [Cimabue believed he held the field in painting, and now Giotto has the cry, so that the fame of the first is darkened. Just so, one Guido has taken from the other the glory of the language, and perhaps he is born who will drive both of them from the nest].

10 Among the scholars in favour of this identification are Ciccuto in "Dante e Bonagiunta," 390–1, and Gorni in "Guittone e Dante," 309–55. Among the scholars against the identification are Barolini in *Dante's Poets: Textuality and Truth in the "Comedy,"* 128n, and Durling in "Mio figlio ov'è? (*Inferno* X, 60)," in Picone, ed., *Dante. Da Firenze all'aldilà,* 320, n44.

11 "E l'un rispuose a me: 'Le cappe rance / son di piombo sì grosse, che li pesi / fan così cigolar le lor bilance. / Frati godenti fummo, e bolognesi; / io Catalano e questi Loderingo / nomati, e da tua terra insieme presi, / come suole esser tolto un uom solingo, / per conservar sua pace; e fummo tali, / ch'ancor si pare intorno dal Gardingo.' / Io cominciai: 'O frati, i vostri mali ...'" (*Inf.* XXIII, 100–9) [And one replied: "The orange robes are so thick with lead that the weights make their balances creak. We were Jovial Friars, and from Bologna, I named Catalano and he Loderingo, and taken both together by your city, though the custom is to take a single man, to preserve the peace; and we were such that it still appears around the Gardingo." I began: "O friars, your evil ..."].

12 "'Oh,' diss'io lui, 'or se' tu ancor morto?' / Ed elli a me: 'Come 'l mio corpo stea nel mondo sù, nulla scïenza porto. / Cotal vantaggio ha questa Tolomea, / che spesse volte l'anima ci cade / innanzi ch'Atropòs mossa le dea'" (*Inf.* XXXIII, 121–6) ["Oh," said I to him, "now are you already dead?" And he to me: "How my body may fare up in the world, I have no knowledge. Ptolomea has this advantage, that often the soul falls here before Atropos has sent it off ..."].

Jovial Friar can legitimately suppose that he, like his brother Knights, is at least a hypocrite, if not an outright traitor.

And what about the invective in canto XXXIII against Pisa, *vituperio delle genti* (shame of the peoples; 79), which was the largest centre of the Knights' preaching? And perhaps we should also mention Stricca, the falsifier of canto XXIX, if he can indeed be identified with Stricca de' Tolomei, Jovial Friar from Siena. But that is by no means all: the *Inferno* is inhabited by other acquaintances of poor Guittone: Cavalcante de' Cavalcanti (canto X), Ugolino della Gherardesca (canto XXXIII), the Conti Guidi (cantos XVI and XXX), and Corso Donati were all among his correspondents. One of the very few people Guittone knew – besides Guido Guinizzelli – who managed to avoid the pains of hell is Judge Nino Visconti, whom we find in canto VIII of *Purgatory*. Although the Pilgrim Dante's surprise at seeing him there is somewhat dubious since he says, "giudice Nin gentil, quanto mi piacque / quando ti vidi non esser tra' rei" (Noble Judge Nino, how I rejoiced to see that you were not among the damned! [53–4]). For Dante, Guittone and his kind unequivocally belong to the world of the damned.

If we continue this line of thinking, it should not come as a surprise that it is in fact Guittone to whom Dante alludes twice in chapter XXV/16[13] of the *Vita nova*.[14] It is difficult not to see the poet from Arezzo among the uncouth and vulgar, the "grossi" mentioned here, who were nevertheless the first poets to use the Italian vernacular and to gain a certain poetic notoriety.[15]

---

13 The traditional division in chapters has been challenged by Guglielmo Gorni's 1996 critical edition: *Vita nova*, ed. G. Gorni.

14 The identification is accepted by Guglielmo Gorni in his critical edition and also by Tristan Kay, "Redefining the 'matera amorosa.'"

15 "E non è molto numero d'anni passati, che apparirono prima questi poeti volgari; che dire per rima in volgare tanto è quanto dire per versi in latino, secondo alcuna proporzione. E segno che sia picciolo tempo, è che, se volemo cercare in lingua d'oco e in lingua di sí, noi non troviamo cose dette anzi lo presente tempo per cento e cinquanta anni. E la cagione, per che alquanti grossi ebbero fama di sapere dire, è che quasi fuoro li primi che dissero in lingua di sí. E 'l primo, che cominciò a dire sí come poeta volgare, si mosse però che volle fare intendere le sue parole a donna, a la quale era malagevole d' intendere li versi latini. E questo è contra coloro, che rimano sopr' altra matera che amorosa, con ciò sia cosa che cotale modo di parlare fosse dal principio trovato per dire d'Amore ..." (*Vita nova*, XXV/16, 4–6) [And not many years have passed since these vernacular poets first appeared; for to write rhymes in the vernacular is as valid, *mutatis mutandis*, as writing verses in Latin. To see that it is a short length of time, we need only research the language that uses *oc* and the one that uses *sì*; in neither do we find poems written more than 150 years before the present time. And the reason that certain coarse individuals were famous for knowing

It would take much less than this collection of accusations to obliterate anyone's literary reputation.

This is not the place to investigate Dante's motivation or to attempt to explain whether or not it was (or still is) justified.[16] What is important to keep in mind, however, is that whenever we read Guittone, regardless of whether we are conscious of it, our attitude is already corrupted by these judgments, which have thoroughly conditioned Italian literary history.[17] And we will have to unburden ourselves completely of this bulky historiographical load if we want to understand precisely what constitutes Guittone's literary greatness. But who was Guittone d'Arezzo?

Guittone's Life (1230/35–1294) and Development[18]

We know very little about Guittone from sources other than his own, or other people's, literary works.[19] He was born in or near Arezzo between 1230 and 1235; he apparently left his city in his twenties to seek his fortune outside of Tuscany; he was in Bologna in 1285; and he seems to

---

how to write poetry is that they were more or less the first to write it in the language that uses *sì*. And the first one who started to write poetry in the vernacular started to do so because he wanted to make his words comprehensible to women who found it difficult to follow Latin verses. This is contrary to those who write rhymes on themes other than love, inasmuch as this mode of composition was from the very beginning invented for writing about love]. And further on: "però che grande vergogna sarebbe a colui che rimasse cose sotto vesta di figura o di colore rettorico, e poscia, domandato, non sapesse denudare le sue parole da cotale vesta, in guisa che avessero verace intendimento. E questo mio primo amico e io ne sapemo bene di quelli che così rimano stoltamente" (*Vita nova*, XXV/16, 10) [For it would be shameful for one who wrote poetry dressed up with figures or rhetorical color not to know how to strip his words of such dress, upon being asked to do so, showing their true sense. My best friend and I are only too well acquainted with poets who write in such a stupid manner]. The English text is given in the translation provided by A. Frisardi in *Vita nova*, ed. and trans. A. Frisardi.

16 For a more detailed analysis of Dante's attitude, see my article "Guittone all'*Inferno*?".

17 We need only recall De Sanctis's merciless comment: "Guittone is not a poet, rather a subtle debater in verse … He is neither a poet nor is he an artist: he lacks the inner sense of measure and harmony that led poets inferior to him in erudition and ingenuity to polish the vernacular … He lacks taste and elegance." In *Storia della letteratura italiana*, ed. Contini, 31 (my translation).

18 A considerable part of this section was originally published as an article of mine on Guittone d'Arezzo in *Encyclopedia of Italian Literary Studies*, ed. G. Marrone, 925–8, and it is reproduced here by permission from Taylor and Francis LLC Books.

19 Guittone's name is very possibly a nickname for the common first name Guido.

have died on 21 August 1294 in Florence.[20] The central event of his life, however, the one around which all of his writings are organized, appears to have been the religious conversion that coincided with the complete rejection of the considerable body of love poetry that had till then been the basis of his fame. Around 1265, Guittone joined the *Milites Beatae Virginis Mariae*, a newly formed religious order popularly known, as a sly commentary on their moderate and tolerant rule, as the *Frati Gaudenti* (The Jovial Friars).[21] At this time, Guittone composed an eighty-six-line *canzone* or ode, "Ora parrà s'eo saverò cantare" ("We will soon find out if I can sing," Egidi, XXV),[22] in which he vehemently retracts and stigmatizes as reprobate and corrupting all poetry inspired by *Amore*, the god of love, especially the poetry he himself had written up to that point. This palinode, composed in the same highly wrought style and complicated rhyme schemes that had characterized Guittone's earlier production, also functions as a manifesto of his new poetry, which will now be devoted to the praise of God and the teaching of Christian values. As a consequence, the three oldest manuscripts that transmit his work (along with the work of the other poets of the *Duecento*) – *Vaticano Latino 3793*, *Laurenziano Rediano 9*, and *Palatino 418* (now *Banco Rari 217*) – all divide his poetic production into two groups, attributing his texts either to "Guittone" or to "Friar Guittone," almost as if they had been written by two different people. The structure of the *Laurenziano Rediano* manuscript is particularly emblematic in this respect. Copied in all probability in the last decade of the thirteenth century in an environment close to Guittone, the codex opens with a group of 41 epistolary texts, 35 by the friar, followed by 434 poems, 232 by the poet from Arezzo, metrically subdivided into *canzoni* and sonnets. The section containing the *canzoni* begins with the above-mentioned manifesto and is followed by 23 other texts all listed under the friar's name. There follow, symmetrically, 24 love songs attributed to "Guittone," and finally 76 poems by other authors. In the sonnet section the order is reversed: the texts attributed to "Guittone" precede the ones attributed to "Friar Guittone." This arrangement creates a somewhat circular structure in which the religious experience encloses, but also orients, the interpretation of the older, pre-conversion,

20 The most complete work on Guittone's life and times remains Claude Margueron's monograph *Recherches sur Guittone d'Arezzo.*

21 In fact, all the documentary evidence on Guittone's life comes from sources of the *Gaudenti* religious order.

22 It is the first of the poems to be found in this anthology (see page 64).

lyrical production. The image that emerges, then, from this manuscript is that of an emblematic Christian life, with a conversion that has in Paul and Augustine its illustrious models. The passionate moral teachings of the converted friar, conveyed by both the letters and the poetry, as well as their repeated condemnations of a sinful past, encourage a reading in autobiographical terms of all of his work, including the poems written before he joined the *Milites*. The love poetry attributed to "Guittone" is thus retrospectively stripped of its original literary autonomy, becoming a mere testimony to an earlier erotically errant version of the self and reinforcing by contrast the sincerity of both his conversion and the moral preachings of the friar. The implicit goodness of the fully embraced Christian doctrine, coupled with Friar Guittone's undisputed poetical mastery, guarantees the moral and literary authority of his teaching. Furthermore, the religious texts establish a continuous dialogue with the older poems, not only through the repeated palinodes, but also by means of a high quotient of references and allusions. Although the *Laurenziano* manuscript was neither compiled nor ordered by the poet's own hand, it may well have been copied from a previous authorial redaction. Two independent sources, a polemical sonnet by Guido Cavalcanti addressed to the friar[23] and an incidental remark made by Dante commentator Benvenuto da Imola, explicitly mention a volume assembled by Guittone. Whether the poet personally prepared a "book" during the last years of his life in which he collected and ordered his production in a form similar to that transmitted by *Laurenziano Rediano 9* is still an object of debate among scholars. Undisputed, however, is the fact that, towards the end of Guittone's life, his poetry must have presented itself as roughly divisible into two parts: one that dealt, like most contemporary lyric poetry, with erotic themes; the other engaged with moral and religious issues, often set in direct opposition to and with the declared intent of making amends for the love poetry. How Guittone's immediate posterity reacted to his legacy is epitomized by Dante's condemnations of his poetry, a critique that, as mentioned before, would exert a powerful negative influence. This devaluation lasted well into the twentieth century, and Guittone was for a long time considered either as a passive imitator of Provençal modes or at best a clumsy precursor of Dante's own moral and political vein. In recent years Guittone's lyric poetry seems to have finally been rescued from Dante's wholesale condemnation and placed in the context of its direct predecessors and models, namely the Provençal

23 "Da più a uno face un sollegismo." See Cavalcanti, *Rime*, ed. De Robertis, 184–6.

troubadours and the poets of the so-called Sicilian School. Several commentators tend to read Guittone's early production, at least partially, as an ironic treatment, from a realistic, bourgeois point of view, of the fashionable love poetry of his day. While northern Italy and the court of Treviso were becoming the main centre for the diffusion and revitalization of Occitan lyric poetry, especially at the hands of Uc de Saint Circ, compiler of most of the Provençal *vidas* and the *razos*, and while the poets of Frederick II's *Magna Curia* had recently proposed the translation and adaptation of selected Provençal modules into the Sicilian vernacular, Guittone's early production seems to take off in a different direction. Far from being an abstract idealization of the behavioural dynamics of the court, with the poet praising an unattainable lady, the source of his inspiration, who grants her favours only in terms of protection and patronage, as was still the case with the Sicilians, Guittone's *Madonna* is instead a credible, real live woman equally skilled in the language of deceit that constitutes the courtly love lyric. Instead of attempting to revitalize the conventions of a genre, possibly adapting it to a new social environment, Guittone operates within the same linguistic and stylistic parameters but wilfully exaggerates those conventions or offers parodies of their clichés in order to demonstrate the ultimate falsity of that language. In a spirit akin to that of the *Roman de la rose*, the rituals of courtly love, in the more down-to-earth context of Italian communal society, are exposed as an elegant pantomime that disguises its real aim, the actual seduction of the lady. This parodic attitude has been shown to be especially evident in the first eighty-six love sonnets transcribed under Guittone's name in the *Laurenziano* manuscript.[24] Thanks to the presence of formal and semantic interconnective devices, the texts may be read as a single sequence in which a character, a poet called Guittone, enters into open debate with the lady whom he is courting. The textual exchange becomes similar to a theatrical representation with overtly comic tones, especially since the suitor's real intentions are eventually revealed, though in the end he is unsuccessful in obtaining the lady's favours.

A somewhat similar stance is to be found in another sonnet sequence, present in this anthology, where Guittone poses as an expert willing to teach his audience how to act in order to seduce a lady. However, more than a real primer for lovestruck men, the sequence can be seen as a parody of the courtly clichés transmitted by troubadour poetry.

24 See d'Arezzo, *Canzoniere*, ed. Leonardi.

Guittone also seems to adopt such a parodic stance in several of his *canzoni,* revealing an author whose ultimate goal is a radical critique of the conventions of the genre from a literary and intellectual bourgeois viewpoint. This attitude is particularly evident in the *canzone* "Se de voi, donna gente" ("It should come as no surprise ...," Egidi, I), anthologized here.[25] The text opens the section dedicated to love songs in the *Laurenziano* and only appears to follow the codified tradition in praising the lady's virtue and the lover's devotion. Upon close examination, it turns out that the text is rather a subtle, persuasive discourse meant to trick the lady into surrendering herself, as the last stanza in particular suggests with its direct request for the lady's favours and its allusion to a possible, paradoxical, and scandalous paid union. Thanks to the *canzone*'s strategic position within the Laurenzian compilation, the text can also be seen as a sort of preface meant to orient the reading of what follows.

Other scholars have tried to show how Guittone's early poetry progressively succeeds in freeing itself from stereotyped courtly modes and already contains *in nuce* the moral preoccupations that will eventually lead to his religious conversion.[26] In this view, the political texts in particular evince the young Guittone's sincere and original ethical disposition. The famous *canzone* "Ahi lasso, or è stagion de doler tanto" ("Alas, now is a time of great suffering," Egidi, XIX), deploring the Florentine defeat at Montaperti (1260), is indeed a powerful example of *sirventes,* the troubadour term for a polemical political text. Another ode, also available here, "Gente noiosa e villana" ("Troublesome, uncouth peasants," Egidi, XV), laments the poet's self-imposed exile from Arezzo where his lady still dwells and fuses themes typical of a "distance song" with harsh criticism of the city's moral and civic decadence.

Undeniably, Guittone's early moral and political poetry is a highly sophisticated literary accomplishment that builds and experiments on the genres already codified by the troubadour tradition.

The Guittonian Corpus

Egidi's critical edition,[27] for all its shortcomings and the difficulties identified by reviewers, Contini first and foremost, remains the only complete

25 The first of the *canzoni* in Egidi's edition (see page 88 and following).

26 See Moleta, *The Early Poetry of Guittone d'Arezzo.*

27 Guittone d'Arezzo, *Le rime di Guittone d'Arezzo,* ed. F. Egidi (1940).

collection of Guittone's poetry.[28] It consists of 24 *canzoni* and 137 sonnets[29] by Guittone (plus one attributed to a mysterious correspondent named Mastro Bandino) and 26 *canzoni* (six of which are religious ballads) and 108 sonnets by Friar Guittone (plus five by correspondents: one each by Guido Guinizzelli, Giudice Ubertino, and Messer Onesto, and two by unknown authors). If we add the only four sonnets certainly by Friar Guittone that the *Giuntina di rime antiche* transmits, the total number is 112.

The situation is different for the corpus of letters, for which we have an excellent critical edition by Claude Margueron,[30] who is also the author of the most important monograph on Guittone, to which I have already referred.[31] His edition contains 36 letters, two of which are written by Meo Abbracciavacca to Guittone. Of Guittone's 34 letters, 31 of which can be attributed to the period after his conversion, six are entirely in verse: VI (to N.N.), VII (to Corso Donati), XI (to the Count of Romena), XV (to Simone), XVII (to Gioane), and XXX (to Marzucco Scornigiano); moreover the prose letters XXVI (to Iacopo d'Architano) and XXXVI (to Messer Ranuccio de Casanova) contain a sonnet and a *canzone* respectively.

The Manuscripts

As with the rest of Sicilian and Tuscan lyric poetry that precedes Dante's *Sweet New Style,* nearly all of Guittone's work has come down to us in three miscellaneous manuscripts, the *canzoniere Vaticano 3793* (V), the *canzoniere Laurenziano Rediano 9* (L), and the *canzoniere Palatino 418,* now *Banco Rari 217* (P). P is located in Florence's Biblioteca Nazionale Centrale and is considered the oldest of the three, safely dating back to the thirteenth century. The manuscript is richly illuminated and prepared by someone who can definitely be said to come from Pistoia, even

28 See Contini's review of Egidi's edition in *Giornale storico della letteratura italiana* 117 (1941): 55–82.

29 The count should also include the 30 sonnets transmitted by the Giuntina, only four of which can be considered to be Guittone's. For the anthology of thirteenth- and fourteenth-century Italian poetry known as Giuntina, actually *Giuntina. Sonetti e canzoni di diversi antichi autori toscani,* see at least the recently reprinted classic study by Debenedetti, *Nuovi studi sulla Giuntina di rime antiche.*

30 Guittone d'Arezzo, *Lettere,* ed. Claude Margueron (1990).

31 Margueron, *Recherches sur Guittone d'Arezzo.*

though the sources he used are from the area of Pisa-Lucca.[32] P contains 180 texts grouped into ten quires and ordered by genre: first the *canzoni,* then the ballads, and finally the sonnets. Not only does Guittone have more texts than any other author; his importance is also highlighted by the fact that by far the largest section of the manuscript (the first eight quires) opens and closes with his *canzoni,* putting into parentheses, as it were, the work of all the other authors, Sicilians included, who do not reach his artistic heights.

The *canzoniere Laurenziano* (L), whose structure and organization by genre (letters, *canzoni,* and sonnets) have already been discussed, most likely dates to the turn of the fourteenth century. Located in Florence's Biblioteca Mediceo Laurenziana with the shelf mark *Redi 9,* this is the quintessential Guittonian manuscript. Of its 474 texts, 274 are attributed to Guittone alone, or as I said above, to both of his *personae,* the love poet and the intellectual spokesperson for the Jovial Friars. This manuscript was compiled by several hands in a context that was very close to Guittone, but it cannot be directly attributed to him.[33] The two principal scribes were both from Pisa, with the first responsible for the majority of Guittone's corpus; there were also two Florentine scribes, who wrote the parts transmitting texts by authors other than Guittone.

The *canzoniere Vaticano*[34] is a rather different affair. It is located in Rome's Biblioteca Apostolica Vaticana with the shelf mark *Vaticano Latino 3793* and is by far the largest and most important collection of lyric poetry marking the origins of the Italian language. This manuscript, which like L probably derives from a common archetype, also dates to the turn of the fourteenth century. V contains nearly one thousand texts divided by genre into *canzoni* (texts 1–325) and sonnets (texts 326–995), and is different in that its ordering is due to a clear chronological and historiographical intention that can be traced to the first and most important of the various Florentine scribes who worked on it.

32 See Rossana Giorgi's article "Analisi linguistica del Canzoniere Palatino," and Valentina Pollidori's "Appunti sul canzoniere Palatino." The illuminations were probably made in Florence; see Giancarlo Savino "Il canzoniere Palatino."

33 See Leonardi's introduction to his edition, *Canzoniere: I sonetti d'amore del codice Laurenziano,* and Bologna, *Tradizione e fortuna dei classici italiani, Dalle origini al Tasso,* 84–90.

34 See Antonelli, "Struttura materiale e disegno storiografico del canzoniere vaticano." See also Giunta, "Un'ipotesi sulla morfologia del canzoniere Vaticano lat. 3793," on the tripartite structure of the *canzoniere canzoni,* sonnets, and *tenzoni.*

The manuscript opens with Giacomo da Lentini, moves on to the so-called Sicilian-Tuscan poets, and ends with the contemporaneous works of the Florentines; Chiaro Davanzati and Monte Andrea are the authors with the greatest number of texts represented. There are 33 *canzoni* by Guittone, of which only five are by the friar, and about 100 sonnets, the vast majority of which also date to the period before his conversion.[35]

The Texts Presented

The ordering of the texts in this anthology mimics the structure of the *Laurenziano*, which starts with the letters, followed by the *canzoni* and the sonnets. Friar Guittone's *canzoni* precede the amorous production, while in the sonnet section the order is reversed. Thus the manuscript not only offers a specular structure, it also encapsulates the erotic production, closed on both sides, both preceded and followed by Friar Guittone's work. In the absence of a trustworthy edition of Guittone's complete lyric production,[36] I selected only *canzoni* for which an acceptable critical text has been established.

As for the text of the 51 sonnets, it is given here in the diplomatic form established for the *Concordanze della lingua poetica italiana delle origini* (*CLPIO*), which presents the poems in the linguistic form that they actually have in the original manuscripts, with their Pisan (L) or Florentine (V) patina, the differences in spelling, and the metrical inconsistencies.

1) The Letters

In this volume I present four of the 34 letters in Claude Margueron's critical edition. Today, Guittone's letters are unanimously considered some of the highest examples of literary prose of the thirteenth century. As with his verse, L is the principal, often the only, manuscript containing the works in question,[37] while V has only one letter (XVII), in verse, addressed to the judge Giovanni dell'Orto. In all likelihood, there are

35 Two quires, VII and VIII, are dedicated to Guittone's songs (texts 132 to 160 are by Guittone, and 161 to 165 are by Friar Guittone). Quire XIX (the second one with sonnets) is entirely for Guittone, with almost 80 sonnets (406 to 480; 471 to 480 are by Friar Guittone). Texts 703 to 721 are also by Guittone.

36 Francesco Egidi's edition, *Le rime di Guittone d'Arezzo*, is considered largely inadequate.

37 Some of the letters are also transmitted by *Riccardiano 2533* (R) and *Laurenziano Conventi Soppressi* (Lk).

other letters by Guittone that have not come down to us; we know for certain of one addressed to the Florentines after the Guelph victory at Campaldino in 1289.[38]

Notwithstanding L's designation of two of the four letters in our edition as by Friar Guittone (V, to the Donna Compiuta, and XIV, to the Florentines), these almost certainly date to the period before his conversion, while XVII, to Marzucco Scornigiano, and XXI, to Orlando da Chiusi, are doubtless works of Friar Guittone. If the overlap of author and narrative voice in the sonnets and *canzoni* of the "amorous" period is often problematic, even when the latter is called "Guittone,"[39] the sender of the letters, both before and after the conversion, is never purely a character. On the contrary, the moral authority that the writer assumes for his teaching comes precisely from the fact of his identification with the intellectual spokesman for the Jovial Friars. His didactic tone, however, cannot obscure the fact that literary models exist, foremost among them the Provençal *ensenhamens* or "teachings" that both Guittone and Friar Guittone refer to, and that the stylistic question most likely precedes any moralistic impulse and permeates the texts, which are conceived as exemplary epistolary models. While strictly adhering to the organizational structure prescribed by the medieval treatises on the art of letter writing (*salutatio, propositio, narratio, conclusio,* and *petitio*), the prose of the letters is characterized by a relatively elevated style that privileges the rhetorical figures of antithesis and *amplificatio.* The letters are constructed with very poetic rhythms, to such an extent that sentences nearly correspond to the stanzas of a *canzone,* and very often mirror Guittone's verse style.[40] Moreover, the alternation of prose and poetry in the letters, and sometimes within the same letter, places them in the literary genre of the *prosimetrum* (a mixture of prose and verse), which is characteristic of the medieval Latin tradition. The high literary model of Guittone's letters had few imitators either in the domains of religious preaching or in the bourgeois style of letter writing. Nevertheless, as Francesco Bruni notes, they earned the distinction of "giving a higher

38 See Guittone d'Arezzo, *Lettere,* xxiv.

39 See for instance s. 29, "Leal Guittone, nome non verteri"; s. 59, "Certo Guitton ..."; s. 208, "Se il nome deve seguitar lo fatto"; s. 209, "Giudice Ubertin, ver son Guittone"; and s. 234. See Leonardi, 1994.

40 See *canzone* XIX (page 112 and following) and letter XIV (page 30 and following), both addressed to the Florentines and both included in this anthology.

meaning to worldly affairs, without however negating what is worldly by despising the world itself."[41]

2) Friar Guittone's Canzoni

In an effort to reproduce the specularity of the principal manuscript containing Guittone's work, I have selected four *canzoni* each by Friar Guittone and Guittone. The friar's work here anthologized consists of two *canzoni* and two religious ballads, a genre that owes its existence directly to Friar Guittone. If "Ora parrà s'eo saverò cantare" ("We will soon find out if I can sing," XXV) is the *canzone* manifesto of a new phase, a palinode of the poetics of the past, one should at the same time highlight the text's rhetorical continuity with the earlier love poems. The extremely elaborate structure of its stanzas, the play of internal rhyme, its taste for puns, and the didactic, rationalistic tone all belong as much to the new period being inaugurated as to the past being repudiated. Moreover, the note of scepticism regarding reason's ability to conquer the passions successfully, which closes the text, makes clear to what extent the converted Guittone's true supreme value derives from the possibility of reiterating his own linguistic talent, rather than from his choice of a new poetic object.

We can also extend this reflection on the objective continuity between the two Guittonian periods to the second text I have selected, "O tu, de nome Amor, guerra de fatto" ("They call you Love, but war is what you are," XXVIII). We might point out that, in addition to taking up troubadour Aimeric de Peguilhan's argument and definitively refusing the notion of love expressed in courtly song, the author uses *interpretatio nominis*, as in "Ahi Deo, che dolorosa" ("Ah Lord, the reason for my song," VII), in order to define the essence of the term he is attacking, and the result is a palinode of the amorous *canzone*.

The two sacred ballads "Vegna, – vegna – chi vole giocundare" ("If she wants to rejoice, let her come," XXXIX) and "Grasiosa e pia" ("Sweet Virgin Mary," XXXV) suggest a rather different reading. Guittone invented this lyric genre, which Jacopone da Todi later glorified, and which basically consists of applying popular ballad metre to an encomium, a song of praise for which the highest metric form (i.e., that of the *canzone*) was traditionally reserved, with the *ritornello* or *refrain* lending

41 See Francesco Bruni's article "Critica della cortesia e poesia etico-religiosa," 1: 317. The English translation is mine.

a hypnotic effect of prayer to the song. The song of the Virgin Mary, who takes the place reserved for Milady in the erotic poems, had obviously already been inaugurated by the Provençal poets, and so once again the poetics of the converted Guittone stand against the backdrop of his Provençal predecessors.

3) Guittone's Canzoni

I have included four of the 24 *canzoni* that Egidi attributes to the years before Guittone's conversion. I have already discussed the importance of the first one, "Se de voi, donna gente" ("It should come as no surprise …," I), and its role in directing us towards a parodic reading of all of his amorous writing. Similarly, I have mentioned that it is impossible to find this same authorial intention in the two political *canzoni* selected: the invective "Gente noiosa e villana" ("Troublesome, uncouth peasants," XV) and the celebrated *canzone* "Ahi lasso, or è stagion de doler tanto" ("Alas, now is a time of great suffering," XIX) on the defeat at Montaperti, which, however, must be read, or reread, against the backdrop of letter XIV, "Ai fiorentini" ("To the Florentines").[42] The fourth *canzone* of love I have included, "Ahi Deo, che dolorosa" ("Ah Lord, the reason for my song"), is one of countless examples in the troubadour tradition of the lover's complaint to his cruel master, the God of Love, whom he accuses of repaying his faithful service with pain and sorrow. I should, however, point out that Guittone's handling of this *topos* on the one hand ties it to the whole problem of the classic equation of love and death, and on the other hand highlights through wordplay (as the love lyrics often do) the substantial referential ambiguity of lyric language. Guittone's conversion was probably first and foremost a literary conversion, but it is also true that years of linguistic experimentation within the entire troubadour tradition led him to genuinely consider the limits of a certain language in the face of his need to resolve his own artistic contradictions in a higher sphere. Not commanding the sophisticated rhetoric of Aristotelian metaphysics, as Cavalcanti and Dante did, should not be imputed to Guittone as a poetic crime;[43] at most we might follow Contini's lead[44] and

42 See Le Lay, "Une lettre pour 'rétracter' après la 'Chanson de Montaperti'?," and the review by Surdich in *Rassegna della letteratura italiana.*

43 See the interpretation of Cavalcanti's sonnet "Da più a uno face un sillogismo" ("From one to many makes a syllogism"), *Rime,* 184–6.

44 Contini, ed., *Poeti del Duecento,* 191.

reconsider the whole debate within the cyclical variations in taste that accompany the emergence of a new generation.

4) Teachings on Love (The Rascal's Manual)[45]

The series of 24 sonnets given in its entirety only in V[46] constitutes an *ars amandi* modelled closely on the teachings of the most famous medieval treatise on the matter, Andreas Capellanus's *De amore.*[47] In a pseudoscientific manner, Capellanus takes up and systematizes all of the commonplaces of the phenomenology of love that can be traced back to troubadour literature, in the hopes of providing the lover with the linguistic instruments and behavioural tips he will need to arrive at his goal. As Avalle notes, the love that Capellanus theorizes is nothing more than the desire for carnal possession, a natural impulse linked to sight, to the beauty of the beloved's body, and to the pleasure that can be had from it, all of which is magnified by the lover's unrestrained excogitations.[48] It is precisely the *immoderata cogitatione formae alterius sexus* (exaggerated thinking about the body of the other sex),[49] the obsessive thinking about the beauty of the other's body, that makes this text innovative with respect to the Ovidian tradition to which it, in turn, owes its existence. We cannot, however, exclude the possibility that Capellanus's treatise is not in fact didactic but rather aims to be a sophisticated, erudite mockery of those very linguistic and behavioural clichés. The palinode of itself to be found in the third book, *De reprobatione amoris* (*Chastising Love*), which also mirrors its Ovidian model, goes some way towards strengthening this hypothesis as well.[50]

---

45 The title was given by D'Arco Silvio Avalle in his edition based on L in *Ai luoghi di delizia pieni.*

46 L preserves only the first ten sonnets in the last quire (texts 362–371), while *Magliabechiano* (M) lacks the first eight.

47 Andrea Cappellano, *Trattato d'amore,* ed. Battaglia.

48 See Avalle, *Ai luoghi di delizia pieni,* 59–60.

49 *De amore,* 4.

50 A recent collection of essays on Capellanus's book and its discordant interpretations is contained in *Immagine Riflessa* N.S. Anno XV (2006) N. 2 (Luglio Dicembre), in Lecco, ed., *Studi sul* De amore *di Andrea Cappellano e sulla sua posterità volgare*; particularly relevant are the essays by Bertini, "Equivoci e doppi sensi nel *De amore* di Andrea Cappellano"; Pittaluga, "Andrea Cappellano e la letteratura d'amore del XII secolo"; and Rapisarda and Croce, "Cinque paradigmi per il *De amore.*" On the irony in the book, see Robertson, "The Subject of the *De amore* of Andreas Capellanus,"

In ways that are analogous to what the future author of *Il fiore* (*The Flower*) would do with the *Roman de la rose*, Guittone's manual offers in an Italian vernacular a concise version of Capellanus's treatise, presumably for an audience that would have difficulty reading his Latin. Posing as an expert, Guittone sets out to teach his audience of lovestruck men how to act in order to realize their goals. He offers practical advice, sometimes brutal in its frankness, whose misogyny nevertheless presupposes a female figure who is well versed in disguising her own carnal intentions, as it takes for granted that she is just as physically motivated as he. Courtship is nothing more than a comedy of deceit where the man plays the role of astute seducer and the woman must preserve appearances rather than her chastity. The devout lover's courtly linguistic equipment must be "translated" so that it is comprehensible, or at least realistic, in an almost exclusively bourgeois cultural context.

Avalle seems to have taken Guittone's little treatise quite literally, thus finding it completely devoid of irony.[51] For him, Friar Guittone's numerous explicit poetic retractions – the sonnet to Monte (V 766), the sonnet "Sì come ciaschuno omo, emfingidore" ("As each man, a pretender," V 469), the *canzoni* "Ahi, quant'ho che vergogni e che doglia aggio" ("Ah, how much should I feel shame and pain," XXVII) and "Altra fiata aggio già, donne parlato" ("Elsewhere, Ladies, I already spoke," XLIX) – are further proofs of the original importance (and perhaps seriousness) of the satanic calling of Guittone's text. Decidedly more convincing for me is Leonardi's theory[52] by which this manual is a sort of parody of Capellanus's treatise. Its apparent seriousness hides the tongue-in-cheek smile of a writer who aims not to teach but rather to amuse an audience of experts on love poetry who are aware that the voice speaking in the poems is merely a mask of someone who certainly does not expect his audience to follow his advice. Even if Capellanus's treatise was in some way a parody itself, Guittone's manual represents less a parody of a parody than a similarly amused and amusing mockery of the abstractions of troubadour language, which can now only be considered "literary" in the worst possible way.

---

and Bowden, "The Art of Courtly Copulation." See also Cherchi, *Andreas and the Ambiguity of Courtly Love.*

51 See Avalle's conclusions, *Ai luoghi di delizia pieni,* 83–6.

52 See Leonardi, *Canzoniere,* xxiii.

5) *The Sonnet Sequences on Vices and Virtues*

As with the *Rascal's Manual*, if we set aside Avalle's diplomatic edition,[53] no critically established text yet exists of the two sonnet sequences that the *canzoniere Laurenziano* (texts 225–51) presents one after the other. What we do have are Egidi's edition and the selection, based on Egidi, that Carlo Salinari made for *La poesia lirica del Duecento*.[54] In these sonnet cycles, from the height of the moral authority that his own conversion and his complete and candid acceptance of religious orthodoxy confer upon him, Friar Guittone shows that his true calling is to teach. Speaking to his brother friars, for whose literary appreciation – read: moral instruction – he had written these poems, Friar Guittone goes through the cardinal sins that lead to damnation and the virtues necessary for the good Christian soul's salvation. The friar dedicates one sonnet to each vice and each virtue, showing off all of his old technical prowess, which, unlike his conversion, is truly above all suspicion. Roberta Capelli is most likely correct when she maintains that the true palinody of the seducer's manual is in the twelve sonnets and one stanza of *settenari* that constitute the *Trattato d'amore* ("Treatise on Love"), to be found only in the *canzoniere Escorialense*, which she expertly edited and published under the title *Del carnale amore* (*On Carnal Love*).[55] But it still may be the case that even these sonnets are a sort of didactic amends that the friar makes, and that they are a quantitative pendant to those very "licentious" sonnets that he wishes to be read as autobiography, just like all of his erotic writings.

What Remains of Guittone Today? Concluding Thoughts

Given what I have so far presented, one might conclude that, considering the manuscript tradition and the various interpretations of his texts, Guittone's poetic activity possibly consists of three phases, with the first two somewhat overlapping. We have a youthful period, as evidenced in *canzoni* such as XVII, XVIII, and XIX,[56] where the author largely seems to be accepting troubadour models. At the same time, however, he starts

53 *Concordanze della lingua poetica italiana delle origini* (*CLPIO*).
54 Salinari, ed., *La poesia lirica del Duecento*.
55 Guittone d'Arezzo, *Del carnale amore*, ed. Capelli.
56 Margueron maintains that these texts date back to Guittone's youth; see *Recherches*, 115–16.

experimenting with hybridizing genres from a bourgeois perspective and demonstrates himself to be critically conscious of the nature of courtly language, of its reappropriation by the Sicilian poets, and of the biographical slant that the troubadours residing at the Treviso court gave it. This consciousness is evident in the sonnets in the *Laurenziano* collection and in a certain psychological stance present in some of the *canzoni.*

Following this is Guittone's conversion and his period of religious moralism, the palinode of his love poetry, and the praise of religious language. Thus we are not only dealing with two Guittones but more likely three: the young troubadour, the bourgeois experimenter, and the converted friar, who are all unified by extraordinary technical mastery and a general didactic and moralistic vocation. If our poet's name is in fact a nickname that refers to some prior vocation as a *guitto* (jester), then we might do well to recall that humorists are also frequently moralists. If Guinizzelli, Cavalcanti, and even the "Notary" surely belong to what our collective imagination has designated as the greatest Italian literary tradition, it is not only for their (undeniable) merits. Dante succeeded in his quest to oust poor Guittone from the place he rightfully occupied in the literary patrimony, and now Guittone's work, but not only his, belongs almost exclusively to the sometimes inaccessible and arcane realm of professional philologists. Perhaps, however, this anthology will go some way towards making the amorous texts in particular more accessible. I hope that a wider audience will be able to perceive and appreciate the subtleties of his language in which playfulness and joyfulness are nearly synonymous. Certainly both Guittone's love lyrics – ironic or otherwise – and his moralistic poems are fundamentally didactic in their tone and their aims. The goal of the lyric poems as well as of the letters is to instruct the reader, but at bottom this instruction has to do with the nature of language. One of literature's most important functions is social, that *docere delectando* which the works of Guittone's pre-conversion period obey, with particular emphasis on the *delectando,* while those of his "new life" move the emphasis squarely onto the *docere.*

It is also of capital importance to recall that Friar Guittone puts all literature on the same pedagogical plane. Classical culture, in which he was not particularly well versed, Christian writings, and the French and Provençal lyrics of the recent past – all are possible instruments for saving the reader's soul, even when the works in question are neither moral nor religious, as is clearly the case with his beloved Peire Vidal.[57] And is

57 See Guittone's letter to Orlando da Chiusi (XXI in Margueron's critical edition), included in this selection, and my note about Peire Vidal (page 50 and following).

this not in fact one of the principal messages that, with all due respect, Dante's *Divine Comedy* imparts?

If Leonardi's hypothesis is correct (and the first eighty-six sonnets of the *Laurenziano* indeed form a *canzoniere*), what survives of Guittone is also, as Corrado Bologna says, "the *form*-book, the *total book*, the book as an instrument able to subsume and condense the totality of an experience," which necessarily anticipated "with the help of the *Vita nuova* the hitherto non-existent pattern of *book-of-life*, of the *book as life*, created, refined, thought out and balanced in its intrinsic relations of tension and force precisely for an entire existence."[58] In other words, the most accomplished *canzoniere*, Petrarch's.

A Note on the Translations

My translations are meant to be as faithful as possible to the letter of the originals, and I have not made the slightest attempt to duplicate in English the extraordinary density of sounds of Guittone's poetry. All the same, I have attempted to produce texts that are aesthetically pleasing to a modern reader. The rhymes, assonances, consonances, alliterations, syntactic inversion, chiasmi, and puns that form the backbone of these poems and that were an inseparable part of the aesthetic experience of Guittone's contemporaries have obviously been sacrificed in this English version, which privileges clarity above all. I nevertheless hope that Guittone's irony, his analogical tendencies, and his taste for reasoning, combined with his implicit and explicit critique of the linguistic conventions of tradition, provide enough reason to appreciate his poetry, especially for those who do not know Italian.

58 Bologna, *L'esperimento di Guittone*, 433–4 (my translation).

Friar Guittone: Letters[1]

1 The texts reproduced here all follow Margueron's critical edition, Guittone d'Arezzo, *Lettere.* They are reprinted by kind permission of the Commissione per i Testi di Lingua di Bologna.

Lettera I[2]

Alla Donna Compiuta[3]

1 Soprapiacente donna, di tutto compiuto savere, di pregio coronata, degna mia Donna Compiuta, Guitton, vero devotissimo fedel vostro, de quanto el vale e pò, umilemente se medesmo racomanda voi.

2 Gentil mia Donna, l'onnipotente Dio mise in voi sì meravigliosamente compimento di tutto bene, che maggiormente sembrate angelica criatura che terrena, in ditto e in fatto e in la sembianza vostra tutta, ché, quanto omo vede de voi, sembra mirabil cosa a ciascun bono conoscidore.

3 Per che non degni fummo che tanta preziosa e mirabile figura, come voi siete, abitasse intra l'umana generazione d'esto seculo mortale; ma credo che piacesse a Lui di poner vo' tra noi per fare meravigliare, e perché fuste ispecchio e miradore, ove se provedesse e agenzasse ciascuna valente e piacente donna e prode omo, schifando vizio e

---

2 The letter is numbered V in Margueron's edition. It is transmitted by both manuscipt L and manuscript Lk. L puts it under Friar Guittone's name, but Margueron maintains that the text was probably written before the conversion, since in the first part, the *salutatio,* destined to bear the greetings and the identification of the sender, the author simply calls himself Guittone and not Friar Guittone as he does in texts written by the friar. According to Margueron the letter is structured as follows: *salutatio* (1), *propositio* (2), *narratio* (3), *conclusio* (4), and *petitio* (5–7).

3 On the identity of the Donna Compiuta, see Margueron, *Recherches sur Guittone d'Arezzo, sa vie, son époque, sa culture,* 173–8, and Guittone d'Arezzo, *Lettere,* 85–7. She must be identified with the author of the three sonnets (510, 511, and 910) transmitted by the Vatican codex 3793. It has also been speculated that the name might be a *senhal,* an alias, that conceals a real woman, if not a man writing under the pretence of being a woman. Margueron's conclusion is that the lady was certainly a laywoman, not a nun, of particular beauty and high moral conduct. Yet the letter can be considered fictitious, a brilliant exercise of style in which Guittone adapts to prose the Provençal poetical genre of the *salutz d'amor* (love salutation), normally in octosyllabic lines, practised, for example by Arnaut de Maruelh, transforming the purely amorous *ensenhamen* of the troubadours into the teaching of a higher spirituality. On this aspect in particular, see Margueron, *Recherches,* 177–8. In her article "Exercices de style pour hypothèses courtoises: Les chansons 1 et 16 et la lettre V de Guittone d'Arezzo," Anne Robin insists on the fictitious identity of the lady and the relation of the letter to Guittone's songs I and XVI. See also the review by Luigi Surdich in *Rassegna della letteratura italiana.*

Letter I

To the Accomplished Lady

1 Most pleasing lady, full of all accomplished wisdom, crowned with merit, my worthy Accomplished Lady, your most devout servant, Guittone, for whatever he is worth, humbly seeks your protection.

2 My gentle lady, almighty God has instilled in you the accomplishment of all that is good. Now you are more like an angel than an earthly creature in both words and deed and in your whole appearance, which seems admirable to every good judge.

3 Since we, the human offspring of this mortal world, were not worthy to live beside such a precious and admirable person as you, it must have pleased Him to place you among us to make us wonder. But also to be a mirror and model of perfection for every gallant woman and man of valour to look at and adorn themselves, shunning vice and

seguendo vertù; e per che voi siete deletto e desiderio e pascimento de tutta gente che vo vede e ode.

4 Or dunque, gentile mia Donna, quanto el Signor nostro v'ha maggiormente allumata e smirata a compimento de tutta preziosa vertute più ch'altra donna terrena, e cusì più ch'altra donna terrena dovete intendere a Lui servire e amare de tutto corale amore e de pura e de compiuta fede.

5 E però umiliatevi a Lui, reconoscendo ciò ch'avete da Lui, in tal guisa che l'altezza dell'animo vostro, né la grandezza del core, né la beltà, né 'l piacere de l'onorata persona vostra non vo faccia obriare né mettere a non calere Lui che tutto ciò v'ha dato;

6 ma ve ne caglia tanto che 'l core e 'l corpo e 'l penseri vostro tutto sia consolato in Lui servire, acciò che voi siate indela corte di Paradiso altressì meravigliosamente grande come siete qui tra noi, e perché l'onorato vostro cominciamento e mezzo per preziosa fine vegna a perfezione de compiuta laude.

7 Ché troppo fòra periglioso dannaggio e perta da pianger sempre mai senza alcun conforto, se per defetto vostro falliste a perfetta e onorata fine.

following virtue. And also because you are the delight, desire, and nourishment of all who see and hear you.

4 Now then, my gentle Lady, as much as our Lord has enlightened and purified you as an accomplishment of all precious virtue more than any other earthly woman, so should you more than any other earthly woman tend towards Him and serve and love Him with all the love of your heart and with pure and accomplished faith.

5 Therefore bow to Him, recognizing what He has given you, so that the perfection of your soul, the greatness of your heart, your beauty, the pleasantness of your honoured person will not lead you to forget or neglect Him who has given you all this.

6 On the contrary, you should take great pains that your heart, body, and thoughts find complete consolation in serving Him. Thus you will be as wonderful in the court of Heaven as you are here among us, and what you honourably started and continued will nobly end with perfection worthy of complete praise.

7 For it would be a dangerously harmful and eternally lamentable loss if you failed to reach a perfect and honoured end through some defect of yours.

Lettera II[1]

Ai Fiorentini[2]

1 Infatuati miseri Fiorentini, omo che de vostra perta perde e dole de vostra doglia, odio tutto a odio e amore ad amore, eternalmente.

2 La pietosa e lamentevile voce del periglioso vostro e grave infermo per tutta terra corre lamentando la malizia sua grande; unde onni core benigno fiede e fa languire di pièta, e nel mio duro cuore, di pietra quasi, pietate alcuna adduce,

3 che m'adduce talento ad operare alcuno soave unguento, sanando e mitigando alcuna cosa suoie perigliose piaghe, se 'l sommo, ricco e saggio bono maiestro mio Dio che fare lo deggia e di fare lo savere donarme degna; ché per me onni cosa in saper è finendo o cominciando alcuno bene.

4 Carissimi e amarissimi molti miei, ben, credo, savete che da fera a omo no è già che ragione in conoscere e amare bene; per che l'omo è ditto animale razionale, e senno più che bestia ha, ch'è ragione. Ragione donque perduta, più che bestia che vale?

---

1 In Margueron's critical edition the letter is numbered XIV. It is transmitted by L only. According to Margueron the letter is structured as follows: *salutatio* (1), *propositio* (2–3), *narratio* (4–48), *conclusio* (49–50), and *petitio* (51).

2 This letter too is to be attributed to the period before Guittone joined the Knights of the Blessed Virgin Mary; Margueron traces the composition to the period 1262–3. The theme is the same as song XIX, "Ahi lasso, or è stagion de doler tanto" ("Alas, now is a time of great suffering"), also anthologized here, and it is a lament for the defeat of the Florentine Guelphs at Montaperti (4 September 1260) at the hands of Florentine exiles, Ghibellines from Siena, and the German troops of Manfred. While the song is full of the hyperbolic sarcasm proper to a political song in the tradition of the Provençal *sirventes*, the letter relies on evangelical teachings, using a much more didactic tone upholding the need for the peaceful solution of the political struggles to the advantage of both body and soul. The letter has been interpreted as a palinode of song XIX; see Leporatti, "Il 'libro' di Guittone e la *Vita nova*." The continuity between the song and the letter is stressed by Le Lay in "Une lettre pour 'rétracter' après la 'Chanson de Montaperti'?" See also the review by Surdich in *Rassegna della letteratura italiana*.

Letter II

To the Florentines

1 Mad, wretched Florentines, I am a man who loses from your loss and suffers from your suffering: hate forever leads to hate and love to love.

2 The sad news of your grave illness is spreading across the land, lamenting its dire state. It wounds and grieves every benign heart with compassion and makes my nearly stone-hard heart feel some measure of pity.

3 It makes me wish to apply a sweet balm to heal and assuage those dangerous wounds. If, that is, my rich, wise and good master God allows me to and gives me the know-how to do it. For me it all depends on being able to finish, or at least begin, something good.

4 Dearest compatriots, you are many and bitter. I think you know that there is no real difference between beast and man except in knowing and loving the good: that is why man is called a rational animal, for he has more intelligence, i.e., reason, than a beast. If he loses reason, how can he be worthier than a beast?

5 Parola di gran saggio[3] vole che "vera perfezione di ragionevole criatura sia per tale com'è avere catuna cosa," cioè in conoscenza e in amore.

6 No è sapienza già che a conoscere bene e amare bono; donque ove si crede e se riceve perdita grande in procaccio, ontosa onta a onore, mortale piaga in salute, no ragione né sapienza, no, ma disragione e mattezza disnaturata dimora loco. Unde vedete voi se vostra terra è cità, e se voi citadini omini siete.

7 E dovete savere che non cità fa già palagi né rughe belle, né omo persona bella né drappi ricchi; ma legge naturale, ordinata giustizia e pace e gaudio intendo che fa cità, e omo e ragione e sapienza e costumi onesti e retti bene. O che non più sembrasse vostra terra deserto, che cità sembra, e voi dragoni e orsi che citadini!

8 Certo, sì come voi no rimaso è che membra e fazione d'omo, ché tutto l'altro è bestiale, ragion fallita, no è a vostra terra che figura di cità e casa, giustizia vietata e pace; ché, come da omo a bestia no è già che ragione e sapienza, non da cità a bosco che giustizia e pace.

9 Come cità può dire ove ladroni fanno legge e più pubrichi istanno che mercatanti? e ove signoreggiano micidiali, e non pena, ma merto riceveno dei micidi? e ove son omini devorati e denudati e morti come in diserto?

10 O reina de la cità, corte di dirittura, scola di sapienza, specchio de vita e forma di costumi, li cui figliuoli erano regi regnando in ogni terra o erano sovra degli altri, che devenuta se'?

11 Non già reina, ma ancilla conculcata e sottoposta a tributo! non corte de dirittura, ma di latrocinio spilonca, e di mattezza tutta e rabbia scola! specchio de morte e forma de fellonia, la cui fortezza grande è denodata e rotta, la cui bella fazione è coverta di laidezza e d'onta, li cui figliuoli non regi ora, ma servi vili e miseri tenuti ove che vanno, in brobbio e in deriso d'altra gente!

12 O che temenza ha ora il perogino no li tolliate il lago? e Bologna che non l'alpe passiate? e Pisa del porto e de le mura? Sia convitato, sia, del mond' ogne barone, e corte tenete grande e meravigliosa, re dei Toscani, coronando vostro leone,[4] poi conquiso l'avete a fine forza!

---

3 The probable source is Guglielmo Peraldo, but see Guittone, *Lettere*, 166.

4 An allusion to the lion kept in a cage in the square of San Giovanni as a symbol of the city, later sculpted and called Marzocco. See Guittone, *Lettere*, 169.

5 A great thinker has said that "the true perfection of rational creatures is to esteem each thing as it truly is"; that is, according to knowledge and love.

6 The only knowledge is knowing and loving the good; therefore, in a place where one suspects and indeed incurs a great loss instead of profit, terrible shame instead of honour, a deadly wound instead of good health, then there is no reason or learning to be found, but only unreason and unnatural madness. So decide for yourselves if your city is a civilized place and if you citizens are in fact reasonable men.

7 You ought to know that palaces and streets do not make a city, nor do physical beauty and rich clothes make a man. Natural law, orderly justice, peace, and joy make a city, and reason, learning, and honest and upright behaviour make a man. I would rather that your city that seems so civilized would not resemble a desert, and that you were citizens and not such dragons and bears!

8 All that is left of man in you are limbs and a general appearance, for everything else is beastly and unreasoned. Likewise, your city has only the appearance of civility and domesticity, for justice and peace are outlawed. Just as man and beast are separated only by reason and knowledge, all that separates civilization from the wild are justice and peace.

9 How can a place where thieves make law and where there are more usurers than merchants be deemed civilized? Where murderers hold sway and receive compensation rather than punishment for killing? And where men are devoured, stripped naked, and killed as in the wild?

10 What have you become, queen of the cities, court of justice, school of wisdom, mirror of life, and model of behaviour, whose children were kings ruling in every land or among the mighty?

11 Queen no longer, but a downtrodden servant forced to pay tributes! Not a court of justice but a den of thievery, a school of all madness and rage! Mirror of death and model of crime, whose great strength has been undone and broken, whose beautiful face is covered with ugliness and shame, whose children are now no longer kings but held to be wretched servants wherever they go, disdained by others!

12 Now why should Perugia fear that you will take Lake Trasimeno from it? And Bologna that you will cross the Apennines? And why should Pisa fear for its port and the city walls? Invite every baron you have defeated with all your might to your grand court to crown your lion King of Tuscany!

13 O miseri miserissimi disfiorati, ov'è l'orgoglio e la grandezza vostra, ché quasi sembravate una novella Roma, volendo tutto suggiugare el mondo? E certo non ebbero cominciamento li Romani più di voi bello, né in tanto di tempo più non fecero, né tanto quanto avavate fatto e eravate inviati a fare, stando a comune.

14 O miseri, mirate ove siete ora, e ben considerate ove sareste, fùstevi retti a una comunitate! Li Romani suggiugòno tutto il mondo: divisione tornati hali a neiente quasi. E voi, ver' che già fuste, tegno che poco siate più che nente e quel poco che siete, credo ben, mercé vostra, ch'avaccio torretel via.

15 Non ardite ora di tenere leone, ché voi già non pertene; e se'l tenete, scorciate over cavate lui coda e oreglie e denti e unghi' e 'l depelate tutto, e in tal guisa porà figurare voi.

16 O non Fiorentini, ma desfiorati e desfogliati e franti, sia voi quasi sepulcro la terra vostra, non mai partendo d'essa, mostrando a le gent' e vostro obbrobbrio spargendo! Ché no è meretrice aldace più che de catuno che n'esce e mostrase, poi la sua faccia di tanta onta è lorda.

17 O desfiorati, a che siete venuti? e chi v'ha fatto ciò che voi estessi? E sembravi forse scusa che no altri havel fatto?

18 Ma mal ragion pensate, che dobbra certo l'onta e 'l fallo, credo; ché primamente a Dio ucidere se stesso l'omo è peccato che passa onni altro quasi; e desnore qual è maggio a esto mondo che arrabire omo in se stesso, mordendo e devorando sé e soi di propia volontà?

19 O desfiorati e forsennati e rabbiosi venuti come cani, mordendo l'uno e devorando l'altro, acciò ch'el poi lui morda e devori! Ché non se stesso strugge e aucide omo, ma strugge e aucide altro, acciò ch'el poi strugga e aucida esso.

20 E se volete dire che vostra intenzione no è già tale, dico che, se non tal è, è fallacie e tenebre vostro lume; ché, come che nessuno serve che per intenzione d'aver merito, non dè omo sì bene provedere alcuno omo che deservito credendo essere apresso, e molto maggiormente e più avaccio e grande mal attender di male che di bene bene avere, perch'è troppo più prunto e solicito omo male che ben rendendo.

13 O most wretched, deflowered Florentines, where are the pride and greatness that made you seem almost like a new Rome, with your will to conquer the entire world? The Romans certainly did not have such noble origins, nor did they accomplish more in the same span of time, nor even as much as you have done and were meant to do if you had remained united.

14 O wretched people, look where you are now, and think about where you would be, if you had governed yourselves civilly! The Romans had conquered the entire world, but division has now reduced them to almost nothing. And in comparison to what you once were, you are a little more than nothing, and I am sure you will soon manage to destroy that little.

15 Would you now dare keep a lion as your symbol, as it is no longer appropriate? And if you did, you would have to cut off its tail, ears, and fur and pull out its teeth and claws for it to represent you adequately.

16 You are not Florentines, but deflowered, defoliated, and broken. I hope your homeland becomes a tomb that you can never leave, spreading your shame for all the world to see! There is no bolder prostitute than all those who issue from your homeland and show themselves in public, for their faces are soiled with such great shame.

17 Deflowered people, what have you come to? Whom do you have to blame but yourselves? And do you think it is an excuse that no one else was responsible?

18 Well, you reason incorrectly, for that surely doubles your shame and guilt, for a man who kills himself commits a sin before God that is greater than almost any other. And what worse dishonour is there in this world than to inflict pain on oneself, willingly devouring oneself and one's own kin?

19 You are deflowered and mad, and you have become as rabid as dogs, inciting each other to mutual aggression! Man does not destroy and kill himself, but others, so that they will in turn destroy and kill him.

20 And if you claim that this is not your intention, then your mind is in darkness and error. Since no one performs a favour without expecting something in return, one ought not to help a neighbour expecting to be badly paid back. Moreover, one should be prepared to receive a greater and quicker evil in return for evil than good in return for good, for we are much quicker in returning evil than good.

21 Ben meritando, è quasi omo avaro rendendo tanto o meno de quel che prende, e le più fiate è tardo; a male de mal rendendo el più avaro par largo, ché non d'uno uno, ma molto, e de' più picciuli grandi; non dè rendere mai male.

22 O che peccato grande e desnatorata e laida cosa offender omo a omo, e specialemente al dimestico suo! Ché non Dio fece omo in dannaggio d'omo, ma in aiuto, e però non catuno vale per sé, ma congregati a uno.

23 No è già fera crudele tanto ch'al suo simile offenda, fòr solamente fere che dimorano coll'omo, come cavallo e cane; e ciò non, credo, appreseno a la lor natura, ma da la malizia dell'omo, coll'omo addimorando, hanoll'appreso.

24 Non unghie né denti grandi diede natura ad omo, ma membra soave e levi, e figura benigna e mansueta, mostrando che non felloce e non nocente esser dea, ma pacifico e dolce, uttulità prestando.

25 E Dio rinchiuse e chiuse solo in caritade e profezia e legge; e chi carità empie, empie onni iustizia e onni bene. E Nostro Signore indela Sua salute[5] non pors'altro già che pace, e finalmente in ultima voglia Sua a li Suoi pace lassò eredità, mostrando che nulla cosa utile è fòr pace, né con essa disutile né nociva.

26 O miseri, come dunque l'odiate tanto? Non conoscete voi che cosa alcuna no amata sa bona, né d'alcun bono gaudere si può fòr pace? Unde onni abitaculo d'omo pacifico esser vorria; ma pur città dico che specialissimo è loco o' gaudio e pace trovare sempre si dea e ove dea refuggire chi gaudio e pace chiere; e s'è loco a guerra reputato alcuno, no è cità, ma alpi, ove alpestri e selvaggi se sogliano trovare omini come fere.

27 Ma a la gran mattezza dei citadini alpe son città fatte, e città alpe, e citadini alpestri in guerra tribulando, e alpestri citadini gaudendo in pace.

28 Isbendate oramai, isbendate vostro bendato viso, voi a voi rendete, e specchiate bene in voi estessi, e mirate che è da guerra a pace; e ciò conoscerete ai frutti loro. O che dolci e delettosi e savorevili frutti gustati avete già indel giardino in pace, e che crudeli e amarissimi e venenosi inel deserto di guerra!

---

5 It is the salutation *Pax tibi* (May the peace be with you).

21 When returning a favour, everyone is hesitant to give back as much or sometimes even less than he has received, but in giving back evil for evil the stingiest person appears prodigal, for we do not return one evil deed for another, but many, and great evil for lesser evils. We should never return evil.

22 It is a great and unnatural sin for one man to offend another, especially a next of kin! For God did not make man so that he could harm others, but to help them; thus, no one is valuable by himself, but only taken with others.

23 No beast is so cruel as to hurt his own kind, except for those that live with man, such as horses and dogs. And I do not think they learned this behaviour from their own nature, but by living with man and seeing his malice.

24 Nature did not give man big claws or teeth, but light, supple limbs and a meek and benign countenance to show that he is neither ferocious nor harmful, but sweet, peaceful, and helpful.

25 God clothed prophecy and law only in charitable love, and he who performs charity, performs every justice and good. And Our Lord put nothing but peace in his salutation, and left peace as His legacy to his disciples to show that no thing is useful without peace, nor useless and harmful with it.

26 O you wretched people, why do you hate peace so much? Do you not know that nothing tastes good unless it is loved, nor can one enjoy any good without peace? Every place man dwells should be peaceful. A city is in fact the place where one should always find peace and joy, and where those who seek peace and joy should take refuge. And if any place is fit for war, it is not the city but the mountains, where both wild and brutish men and beasts are found.

27 But because city dwellers have lost their minds, the mountains have become cities, and cities mountains; city dwellers have become uncivilized and are embroiled in war, while mountain men have become civilized and rejoice in peace.

28 Now remove the blindfold from your eyes, return to yourselves, and look carefully within you. See what difference there is between war and peace by looking at their respective fruits. O what sweet, delectable fruits you have enjoyed in the garden of peace, and what cruel, bitter, poisonous ones you tasted in the desert of war!

29 Che gustare li potete è meraviglia, e sembravi fagian' i' savore, e ve pascete in essi. Per che pare esser malato forte palato de vostro core, ch'a lo sano sa meglio buccella secca in pace ch'ogni condutto in guerra, e voi ha più savore in guerra buccella secca che 'n pace onni vivanda.

30 O chi vi move a cosa tanto diversa? Ditelmi, se vi piace, in vostra iscusa; ché natura né legge né alcuno uso bono né ragion né cagione, pro né onore vostro né gaudio vedere ci so. E se dire me volete che pregio e piacere sia grande voi danneggiare e desfare vostri nemici, dico che ciò è vero, ma vi dimando chi vostri nemici sono. E se mi dite vostri vicini, nego in tutto e dico che non son già.

31 Nemico all'omo no è che nociva cosa, e cosa nociva no è che peccato; peccato alcuno non prende ove non vole; donque a ragione dell'omo nemico è solo peccato. E se solo è nemico, solamente è da odiare; unde se lui odiate e destruggete, odiate e destruggete vostro nemico; e io molto vel lodo. Ma se odiate e destruggete omo, odiate e destruggete voi; e ciò si mostra per plusor ragione, de le quale alcuna assegno.

32 Prima dico che non onore, non prode, non onta né danno alcuno hanno vostri vicini, non voi in comune abbiaten parte. Secondo dico: chi sono vostri vicini? Non sono nati di voi e voi di loro? Perché d'un sangue e d'una carne siete, no è alcuno in parte, non in l'altra parte aggia plusori de sangue e d'amore seco congiunti, cui danno, cui onta e cui dolore participa, voglia o no.

33 E se tutto ciò pregiate poco né di loro non sentite, pregiate e sentite almeno di voi; ché se bene li occhi aprite e vostro viso è chiaro, non vederete antica o novamente esser devenuto che terra a terra offendesse, omo a omo, unde non fusse alcuno tempo vendetta.

34 E se ciò non vedete in altrui bene, almeno mirate voi; e non credo che già troviate guàire che parte a parte, omo ad omo desse una che non presa aggiane un'altra o forse due; ché se vostri vicini donâr già voi, non doglion già de non bon pagamento, ché capitale e merto rendete loro, e assai ben suficiente, via, credo più non fu loro intenzione;

29 It is astonishing that you can savour the fruits of war, feeding on them as if they were exquisite pheasants. The palate of your heart must be very ill indeed, for to a healthy one a mouthful of dry bread in peacetime tastes better than any delicacy in war, and to you a mouthful of dry bread in wartime tastes better than any delicacy in peace.

30 Who brings you to such a strange pass? Please tell me, by way of excuse. For I can see neither nature, nor law, nor any good custom, nor good reason or cause, nor profit, nor honour to you, nor joy in your action. And if you tell me that it is a great prestige and pleasure to destroy your enemies, then I say that may be true, but ask you who your enemies are. And if you tell me that they are your fellow citizens, I reply that they are nothing of the sort.

31 Man's only enemy is that which is harmful, and sin is the only thing that is harmful. No one is contaminated by sin against his own will; therefore, sin is the only enemy to man's reason. And if it is our only enemy, it is the only thing we should hate. If you hate it and destroy it, you hate and destroy your enemy, and that is praiseworthy. But if you hate and destroy another man, you hate and destroy yourselves. This is evident for many reasons, some of which I will now mention.

32 First, your fellow citizens are privy to no honour, profit, shame, or harm whatsoever that you are not also privy to. Secondly: who are your fellow citizens? Are they not born of you and you of them? Since you are of the same flesh and blood, there is no one in either faction who is not related by blood and love to many people in the other. And whether he likes it or not, he is privy to their harm, shame, and pain.

33 And if you do not value any of this and feel nothing for them, at least value and feel for yourselves, for if you open your eyes wide, you will not find in the recent or distant past that any city or man has offended another, without someday eliciting vengeance.

34 And if you do not see this in others, at least look at yourselves. Moreover, I do not think there is a single example of one faction or of one man offending another without at least once or twice suffering reprisal. For if your fellow citizens ever gave you offence, they do not complain of having been poorly repaid, that you return both capital and interest, and quite a bit more, I believe, than what they intended.

35 e forse non credete ei rendan voi; ma ingannati siete, se mantenete lo gioco lungamente, ché finalmente voi essi consumerete e essi voi, come dui baratteri l'uno consuma l'altro al gioco, giocando lungamente.

36 Unde dico, tutto contra Dio fusse e contra giustizia, e disavere, prender vendetta l'omo, serebbe alcun rimedio e mattezza e fallo assai menore offender l'omo e fare vendetta, se sicurtà avesse de non prenderne merto; ma creder si può, sì come è al certo riavere d'una una o forse più; come ferire ardisce e sé non guarda?

37 E però dico voi, se ragione e cagione aveste molta di confondere l'uno l'altro, se non timore e amore del Signor Nostro, né sangue umano e dimestico ten voi, tegnavi almeno timore e amore de voi estessi e de vostra famiglia.

38 Ché gli antichi padri e madre vostre, che di travaglio loro in sicurtà, in pace e gaudio posare vorriano, in guerra e in dolore e in paura languire e penare fatti li avete e correre cià e là di terra in terra.

39 E mogliere vostre, che morbide sono e grave, che posando e pascendo bene doveano demorare inele sale e inle zambre vostre tra i dimestichi loro, pasciute e vestite male, e sole come ancille, e male acompagnate alcuna fiata, di loco in loco andate tribulando, in magioni laide e strette, tra masnade tal fiata e con istraina gente a dimorare, sì che l'ancille altrui eran loro quasi donne.

40 E a' figliuli, a cui padre dea magione adificare, conquistare podere e procacciare amore con pace loro, l'altrui magione strugge, acciò ch'omo la loro strugga. Podere spendete e consumate in guerra, e ucidete altrui, che quasi pegno è loro d'essere ucisi.

41 Ahi, che pessima eredità lassate loro! Certo non padre già, ma annemici tener posson voi, ché struggimento e morte lor procacciate. Ben dèno rifiutare a padre voi, e nel sepulcro ispogliarsi a vostra fine, rifiutando voi e onni vostro. Consanguinei e amici vostri a forza mettete in briga, e procacciate loro danno, travaglio e odio.

42 Se a padri e a moglieri e a figliuoli e ad amici danno tenete in guerra e anco a voi stessi, a cui donque valete? Certo a' demoni molto e a

35 Perhaps you do not believe that they will seek retribution; but you are mistaken, if you keep playing this game long enough, for in the end you will ruin each other, just like two gamblers who wear each other out by gambling over a long period.

36 Therefore, if seeking revenge were a folly against God and justice, it would be a much lesser folly, fault, and solution to offend a man and get revenge, if one were sure of not having to pay interest. But since one will surely incur one or more forms of vengeance for every offence, how could anyone think of harming another without protecting himself?

37 Which is why I say that if you had good reasons for mutual destruction, and neither the fear nor love of Our Lord, nor human or familial blood could hold you back, the fear and love for yourselves and your family ought to.

38 Your aging fathers and mothers would like nothing better than to rest from their labour in safety, peace, and joy. But you have made them languish and suffer in war, in pain, and in fear, and chased them all over from one land to the next.

39 And your wives should have rested and nourished themselves at home, surrounded by their kin. But they are weak and pregnant, poorly fed and clothed, lonely as servants amidst bad company, for you have made them wander desperately from place to place, living in narrow, dirty houses among strangers and criminals. And by comparison, the servants of others seemed to them to be almost like ladies.

40 And what of your sons? A father should build them a home, acquire property, and provide them with both love and tranquillity. Instead, you destroy the homes of others, inciting them to destroy those of your children. You squander your wealth on war and kill others, almost sealing your children's fate.

41 Oh, what a terrible legacy you leave to them! They ought to think of you as enemies rather than fathers, for all that you give them is destruction and death. They have good reason to repudiate you as fathers, and on the day of your death they should refuse your legacy, disowning you and all that belongs to you. You force your next of kin and your friends into great torment, which gains them only harm, suffering, and hate.

42 If you harm your fathers, your wives, your children, your friends, and even yourselves through warfare, whom then do you benefit? Most

catuno che vole lo danno e l'onta vostra, ché spessamente gauder di voi li faite. Amici donque a nemici, e a nemici più chi più v'ama. E ciò poi conoscete apertamente, ché pur donque seguite?

43 E se alcuno è intra voi che pure guerra li piaccia, piacciali ad opo suo: non tutti il seguite a morte vostra; ché ben credo de voi la maggio parte, che pur perdeno sempre ed han perduto: quale che perda o vinca, onni perde vincente ed esconfigge perdente; perden d'onni guerra e riceveno vittoria d'onni pace.

44 E credo tali e tanti a cui avene, che, s'elli volesser bene, malgrado a cui pesasse, sconfiggereano in buona pace chi loro sconfigge in guerra; ma sembra che siano infatuati, lor morte permettendo ante lor viso. E s'elli dicono: "Ma vorremmo e non potemo," dico dicon non vero.

45 Catuno salvar sé vole, ma no procacciare come si salvi. Se vollesseno la lor comune pace, come vole ciascuno lo ben suo proprio e come ad esso acquistando veglia e pensa e fa quant'el può far com'ello sia, serebbe in pace avere, e faccendolo sì bene, non già dotto che fallir potesse.

46 Qual è cosa sì dura che grande e ferma voglia e sollicita e saggia operazione non ben finisca? Ma vostra voglia è vile e debile molto; e pare che catuno dica: "Non tocc' a me; e se mi tocca, non tanto ch'e' vogliame travagliare."

47 O miseri voi, e ciechi, che cosa vi pertene più? Non pende in ciò anima e corpo e onor tutto vostro e 'l pro? In ciò che vale quanto avete, anima e corpo e figliuoi vostri, è danno. No è ciò tutto invano, che son posti presso ciò a perire in guerra?

48 O quanti ne sapete istrutti e morti, che non sel pensâr già a ciò venire! e quanti anche hane intra voi di tali che dottan poco che in vostra guerra perirano, se dura! E però non s'infinga alcun omo d'iscampare li suoi e sé. Non dican, no: "Non è mio fatto," ché suo fatto è ben tale. Onni suo fatto è fatto, se non fa esso; e se fa esso, rifatto.

likely demons and everyone who wishes you harm and shame, for you make them happy so often by your conduct. You should consider your friends as enemies, and those who love you the most as your worst enemies. And since you clearly know what you are doing, why do you persevere?

43 And if there is someone among you who loves war all the same, let him love it for his own advantage, but do not all follow him to your death. I am convinced that the great majority of you always lose and have always lost. Regardless of who appears to win or lose in war, all winners in reality lose and all losers triumph, and both are defeated by every war and receive victory from every peace.

44 And I believe that if those to whom these things happen sought their own advantage, regardless of some people's displeasure, they would use peace to defeat those who defeat them in war. But they seem quite mad, for they allow their own death to hover before their eyes. And when they say that they would like to do this and yet cannot, they are not telling the truth.

45 Everyone wants to save himself but does not want to devise a way in which to do so. If people wanted mutual peace, they could have it. For everyone wants his own good and stays vigilant and provides for it and does all that is possible to that end. And if everyone worked towards peace with as much energy, I have no fear that the effort would not succeed.

46 What could be so hard that a firm resolve and wise and persistent effort would not eventually be able to crack it? Your desire is base and weak. It seems as if you are all saying: "I am not responsible, and if I am, it is not so important that I would want to work hard for it."

47 You blind wretches, what could concern you more than this? Do your soul, your body, and your entire honour and profit not depend upon it? Everything that you have of value – your soul, your body, and your children – is in danger. Is this not all in vain when you put them at risk through war?

48 How many people do you know who have been destroyed or killed who never thought they would come to this! And how many among you are scarcely afraid of dying in your war, if it persists! No one should fool himself that he will be able to save himself or his kin. No one should say: "This does not concern me," for it does. Everything we leave undone is done by others, and everything we do is done again.

49 Piacciavi donque, piaccia ormai sanare, e no schifare medicina amara, che tanto amara malatia vi tolle. Bono spendere è denaio che soldo salva, e bono sostener male che tolle peggio; e moneta con angostia non poco costa voi a conquistare la vostra infermitate, e non meno vi costa a mantenerla.

50 E che mattezza maggio che solicito e largo esser omo in accatar male, e negrigente e scarso bene acquistando? Vinca, vinca ormai saver mattezza; e se non pietate ha l'un de voi del mal grave dell'altro, àggialo almen del suo, e per amor di sè partasi da male.

51 Ciò che ditt'aggio e che dir pore' anco in questa parte, vi conchiudo in uno sol motto, cioè: catuno ami ben se stesso e viv' a sta salute.

49 So you must try to recover and not avoid your bitter medicine, for you have fallen victim to a bitter illness. It is good to spend money if it saves you money, and good to endure an evil that prevents a worse evil. And it will cost you no small amount of money and pain to conquer your ill, but it will not cost you less if you persist in your ways.

50 And how much greater a folly is it to be quick and generous in acquiring evil and negligent and stingy in acquiring good? Let wisdom now vanquish madness, and if you have no pity for the evil another performs, at least have pity for your own. And for the love of yourselves, leave evil behind.

51 I can sum up in one sentence all that I have said and could still say about this matter: let everyone truly love himself and follow this healthy rule.

Lettera III[1]

A Marzucco Iscornigiano[2]

1 Nobele molto e magno seculare, d'amore e d'onore fabricatore, messer Marzucco Iscornigiano, Guittone, vilissimo e picciulo religioso ai piedi de vostra altezza mette se stesso.

2 Dogliomi che sono solo de voi dolendo, ché catuno omo vi pregia. Se dispregiar vi voglio, no ha già loco; e forse che volenteri vi pregeria, non la lingua avesteme impedita.

3 E come vi deggio dire, dico che, come credo a voi sovegna, nel tempo che fuste assessore d'Arezzo, Viva de Michele, lo quale fo detto mio padre, camarlingo fue del Comune e me vedeste picciul garzone molte fiate servi· lui in Palazzo.

4 Unde esso, per la gran lealtà vostra e bonitade e devozione ch'avea in voi, in alcuno vostro bisogno improntò voi libre cento, sì come io ricordo e trovai iscritto per la man sua.

5 E partito d'esta vita esso, io feci procuratore e mandai recherendo voi essa moneta; e come che voi foste impedito d'altro, non vi gradio di darla; e io poi nigrigente non più la chiesi.

---

1 In Margueron's critical edition, the letter is numbered XVIII. It is transmitted by both L and Lk. According to Margueron the letter is structured as follows: *salutatio* (1), *propositio* (2), *narratio* (3–11), *conclusio* (12), and *petitio* (13).

2 Like his father, Gaetano, Marzucco [I]Scornigiano was a judge and a very prestigious and authoritative public figure of Pisa playing an important political role in both Tuscany and the Marches. He was *assessore* to the Podestà in Arezzo in 1249, a tenure to which the letter refers. Born probably between 1210 and 1215, Marzucco joined the Franciscan order in Pisa as a novice before April 1286. On that occasion Guittone wrote him a long letter in verse (XXX in Margueron's edition), highly praising his renunciation of the world and recommending humility as the best virtue to practise in the service of God. He died between 1298 and 1301. In this letter Guittone emphasizes the *topos humilitatis* in order to remind the noble and powerful addressee of an outstanding monetary debt that Marzucco contracted with Guittone's father and at the same time to offer his services to the illustrious Pisan, most likely in an attempt to strengthen the ties of the Jovial Friars with the government of Pisa (see Margueron, *Recherches sur Guittone d'Arezzo, sa vie, son époque, sa culture*, 228–30, and Guittone, *Lettere*, 199 and 298). During the last years of his life, Marzucco's presence can be traced in Florence at Santa Croce, where Dante might have met him. He is mentioned in *Purgatorio* VI, 16–18, as the "buon Marzucco."

Letter III

To Marzucco Iscornigiano

1 Sir Marzucco Iscornigiano, great and noble man of the world, maker of love and honour, Guittone, a most humble and insignificant man of the cloth, puts himself at the feet of your highness.

2 It pains me to be the only one who complains about you, since everyone else praises you. There is no reason for me not to praise you, and I would gladly do so, had you not given me cause.

3 And since I must, I will tell you that, as you no doubt remember, when you were judge in Arezzo, Viva de Michele was the Town treasurer. It was said he was my father and you knew me as a humble young man often helping him out at court.

4 In this capacity, and because of your great loyalty and goodness and for the devotion he had to you, he lent you one hundred pounds for a certain need of yours. This I remember and also found written in his own hand.

5 And when he departed from this life I became his executor and I sent you a request for that money. But since something else prevented you, you did not see fit to return it, and subsequently I neglected to ask for it again.

6 Ma voce di vostro pregio che mi fiere a l'oreglie, e ricordanza de ciò ch'assegnato fuste e menato ad Arezzo per lo più leale omo de vostra terra, e ne l'oficio crevve la fama vostra, me conforta e me punge a dimandarla voi anco.

7 E si, come io dissi, catuno vi loda per leiale e discreto e valente omo, e a mio opo perdeno operazione le ditte vertù in voi, reputeròlo defetto vostro? Non già certo, ma mia mesaventura e mio peccato, che fatto endegno m'ha non solamente di ricevere grazia, ma meritata cosa.

8 E se ciò seguerete, sadisfarete me tardi. Ma io richieggio la vostra gran bonità che v'adduca operando in me sovra de me, non me ma voi guardando; ché, perch'io non sia degno recevitore, voi pur siete degno debitore e datore.

9 E se mi dimandate che contratto e che prova di ciò vi mostro che dico dovete, dico che contratto non fu già fatto che per mancanza di fede o de memoria;

10 per che, secondo ciò, non intendo che facciame misteri avere in carta scritto ciò che pinto voi credo in memoria, ché prod' omo non obria mai beneficio; né infedele vi deggio pensare né oso contra la comune oppinione e opera manifesta.

11 E però, caro messer, contratto del mio dimando vostra memoria assegno, avocato mio vostra coscienza, iudice tra noi vostra discrezione e vostra lealtà grande ditenitrice di voi, stringendovi a me pagare.

12 A pena che vedeste anco, messer, meglio apparecchiato omo in alcun piato; unde vincere pur credo per la mano vostra.

13 Ma se pur piace voi che perder deggia, vinto de ciò me chiamo; e non solamente essa moneta più vi dimando, ma l'altra, che m'è remasa e m'è appresso, prometto al piacere vostro, servendo voi; ché 'l pregio del valor vostro m'ha sì congiunto a sé, non può me despiacere cosa che piaccia a voi voler de me.

6 But news of your reputation comes to my ears and I remember that you were nominated and led to Arezzo for your great loyalty to the city, and in fact your fame grew while you were in office. All this comforts and prompts me to ask you for that money again.

7 And since everyone praises you as a loyal, virtuous, and valorous person, and yet those virtues are of no help to me, should I see this as a defect on your part? Of course not: my misfortune and my sins have made me unworthy not only of receiving favour, but also of deserved compensation.

8 All the same, you should consider repaying me later rather than never. I ask that your goodness lead you to behave towards me as if I were greater than I am, taking into consideration not me but yourself. For even if I am not a worthy recipient, you are nevertheless a worthy debtor and benefactor.

9 And if you should ask what contract and what proof I can show you of your debt to me, all I can say is that a contract was never made up if not to replace an oversight of faith or of memory.

10 As such, I do not think I need a document stating what I believe is painted in your memory, for an upstanding man never forgets a good turn done him, nor should I think you unfaithful or dare to go against your accomplishments and public opinion.

11 For this reason, my dear sir, I call upon your memory for the contract of my request, I take your conscience as lawyer, your discernment as judge, and your loyalty as the obligation to pay me.

12 It is difficult to imagine that you have ever seen anyone with such a strong case, therefore, I believe I can win with your judgment.

13 Yet if you should wish that I lose, I declare my defeat, and not only will I never again ask for that money, but I promise to leave everything else I have to your discretion to better serve you. I am bound by the fame of your great worthiness that I cannot dislike anything you may want of me.

Lettera IV[1]

A Orlando da Chiusi[2]

1 Creditor di pregio e d'amor molto, ser Orlando da Chiusi, Guitton, tutto non degno ditto frate intra i frati cavalier di Beata Maria, pazienza in aversità e gaudio in tribulazione, in acquisto di vita eterna.

2 Carissimo padre mio, non pò leggeramente corpo grave turbare, non turbi lo 'ntelletto, né lo 'ntelletto, non vigore di pazienza manchi: ove si mostra alquanto la miseria grande de l'umana natura nostra, che, quanto maggiormente bisogno ha di valere, val meno; unde avvene che quale è vigoroso e saggio più, se medesmo non consigliare sa bene a tempo d'aversità.

3 Unde io dottando, padre, che per lo gran turbamento del corpo vostro no lo 'ntelletto e 'l vigore dell'animo sia turbato, no insegnando movo, rapresentando ai sotili occhi turbati de vostra mente alcuno prezioso unguento, sanando e mitigando le piaghe vostre, del quale sovente avete e voi e altri sanato.

4 No è già, caro padre, da dubitare che cara sovr'onni cara cosa non sia vertù; unde Tulio dice: "Tutte cose altre cadevele e vane sono, che solo una: vertù de la radice de l'Altissimo radicata"; e quanto più, più è da desiderare e da cherere. Intra gli altri modi, aversità è quella ne la quale si chere, s'affina e se conosce.

---

1 In Margueron's critical edition, the letter is numbered XXI. It is transmitted by L alone. According to Margueron the letter is structured as follows: *salutatio* (1), *propositio* (2–3), *narratio* (4–30), *conclusio* (31–4), and *petitio* (35).

2 Orlando was the son of the nobleman who donated the Monte della Verna to St Francis of Assisi. He was an important feudal lord to whom Guittone also addressed two of his songs, "Ora che la freddore" ("Now that the cold weather," XVIII), with which the letter has many points in common, and "Chi pote departire" ("Who can depart," XLIV). The letter, written by the friar, must be read against the backdrop of the first song, written at a much earlier date (see Margueron, *Recherches sur Guittone d'Arezzo, sa vie, son époque, sa culture*, 246–50, and Guittone, *Lettere*, 225–6). The song urges Orlando not to be defeated by adversity, and so does the letter, which relies on the accumulation of *exempla* taken from medieval *compendia*. The letter, however, also provides us with precious insights into Guittone's (and Orlando's) literary preferences, especially among the troubadours.

Letter IV

To Orlando da Chiusi

1 I, Guittone, owe you praise and much love, sir Orlando. Even though I am unworthily called a friar among the friar knights of the Blessed Mary, let there be patience in adversity and joy in tribulation, in order to acquire everlasting life.

2 My dearest father, seldom does the body suffer gravely without the intellect also suffering in equal measure, nor can the intellect be troubled when the strength of patience is not lacking. The great misery of our human nature is evident in this, for the more it needs to prove its valour, the less worthy it is. And it so happens that the stronger and wiser cannot counsel themselves appropriately in times of adversity.

3 Therefore, father, since I fear that your intellect and the vigour of your soul are troubled due to the great trouble of your body, I am compelled not to teach but to evoke a precious balm for your mind's eye. This balm, which you often used to heal yourself and others, will assuage and heal your wounds.

4 One should not doubt, dear father, that virtue is a precious thing, more precious than anything else. As Cicero says: "All things are fleeting and vain except that virtue which is rooted in the root of the Most High." And the stronger it is rooted, the more it should be desired and sought after. Adversity is the path by which virtue is to be sought after, refined, and known.

5 Dice Aristotile in *Etichi* che "vertù no è già che 'ntorno grave cose." E io non veggio già om che 'n piacer seggia e in agio, chedere e invenire vertù: quanto ha d'agio più om, meno li tocca bisogno, e quanto meno li tocca, men se move a valere;

6 unde: "Poso," dice Bernardo, "di tutti vizii è sentina"; ché come bisogno crea e fa vertù, crea poso peccato. Dice alcun saggio: "Nullo semigliame più misero che quello a cui nulla vene d'aversità," ché "saprà qual è, né esso né altri."

7 Unde dice che molti, cessando briga d'essi, briga orrata chedeno, mostrando sé e altri ciò che vagliano e venendo a vertù, vertù usando; ché, come dice Aristotile: "Vertù se fa per uso bene operando." Dice beato Gregorio: "Chi non tentato che sa?" E dice che "continua temporale consolazione è segno d'eternale reprobazione."

8 E dice nel *Troiano* Agamenone, imperadore de' Creci:

"Chi non ha guerra né aversità
né dannaggio né povertà,
come conoscerà el suo valore?"

9 Come può, come, padre, valore e senno de nochieri parere, che 'n tempestoso mare e torto vento? e come fermezza de castello, che 'n destro e poderoso assedio e forzo? e come valor de prod' omo, che en grande aversità e in periglio? Non ben provase scudo a la caviglia pendendo, ma in braccio di forte cavalieri a colpi grandi di ferme aste e di trincianti ferri. Tutta fortezza stae in non pregiare averse né prosperevole cose.

10 Dice Macrobio: "Fortezza è animo sopra periculi operare, e non cosa temere altra che laida, e prosperevole e averse cose sostenere forte." Dice in *Etichi* Aristotile: "Fortezza è fuggire ch'è da fuggire, e da seguire, seguire"; e dice ch' "esta vertù s'accatta non pregiando terribile cose"; e dice: "ché feminil è fuggire molestevole cosa."

11 E però, padre mio, pugnate forte, ché chi non combatte non vince; e chi non vince, come vittoria prende? E non meno conta saggio vittorevile vinta in tribulazione vincere che 'n battaglia; in battaglia trova altri assai de pro', in tribulazione pochi o niente, perché 'n tribulazione vince om sé, che sopra onni vittoria è preziosa.

5 In the *Ethics* Aristotle says that "There is no virtue where there is no adversity." And I have never seen a comfortable, satisfied man seeking and finding virtue. The more comfortable a man is, the fewer things he needs and the less he is spurred to be valiant.

6 Therefore, "Leisure," says Bernard, "is the breeding ground of all vices." For as need creates virtue, leisure creates sin. A wise man has said that: "The most miserable of men is he who receives everything without difficulty," since "he will not know what his worth is, nor the other's."

7 It is often the case that those who are freed from one form of trouble seek out some honourable difficulty to demonstrate their worth, to acquire virtue by practising virtue. For as Aristotle says: "One becomes virtuous through the exercise of good." And the Blessed Gregory says: "Who can acquire knowledge without knowing temptation?" And again, "constant worldly consolation is a sign of eternal damnation."

8 And in the *Roman de Troie*, Agamemnon, emperor of the Greeks, has this to say:

> "How will a man know his worth
> if he knows not war, adversity,
> damage, poverty?"

9 Father, where can a pilot show his valour and wisdom if not on a stormy sea against an unfavourable wind? And how can a castle show its solidity but under a powerful siege and attack? And how can a courageous man show his valour if not in great adversity and peril? A shield does not prove its value hanging from a hook, but on the strong arm of a horseman against the blows of javelins and swords. Strength comes from not overrating what is either adverse or advantageous.

10 Macrobius says: "Fortitude is to act courageously against perils, and not to fear anything but what is shameful, and bravely to face prosperity and adversity." In the *Ethics* Aristotle says: "Fortitude is to flee what must be fled, and to follow what must be followed." And also that "one acquires this virtue by not fearing terrible things"; and again: "it is effeminate to flee what is harmful."

11 Therefore, my father, fight vigorously, for one does not win without fighting. And how can one gain victory without winning? A wise man does not consider a complete victory over one's hardships to be a lesser victory than one gained in battle. In battle one has many courageous helpers, while in hardship, few or none, for a man must conquer his hardships alone.

12 "Non in mare, non in periculo solamente," dice beato Geronimo, "par vertù, ma appare nel letto" e in periglio d'enfermitate, ove onni vertuoso desvertuda e perde quasi corona de pazienza e de vertù. E quella è vertù grande vincere o' perdeno altri, che quale vince tutti è più forte de tutti.

13 E però dico, padre, che quello è maggiormente da pregiare che 'n aversità provasi meglio. Come 'l foco mostra di che valuta è l'auro, mostra tribulazione di che vertù è l'omo, e quasi come foco è proprio auro affinando, è propia tribulazione affinando omo.

14 Unde Agustino: "Fornace de tribulazione legna de vizii incennera e auro de vertù purga." E però dico che no è cosa mai più da fuggire che quieta consolazione, ove valor si perde, né più da cherere che bisognevele angostia, ove s'acquista, ché, se non vale, a valere lo permove, e s'el vale, el permove e 'l megiora.

15 Come vole sperone malvagio e buono cavallo, e punto e affannato esser rechere, similmente vole omo; come in poso troppo acquista vizii, valore e bontà perde simel om.

16 Unde Cristiano[3] là dove Allessandro Novello dice:

"Reposo e loda
non concordano bene insieme."

17 Dice alcun Provenzale:[4]

"A bel mangiare e a giacere molto soavemente
pò l'omo stare malvagio,
ma chi bon pregio vol mantenere
carcato è d'affanno grande;
misteri gli è procacciare cià e là
e tollere e dare come convene
e vole tempo e ragione."

---

3 It is Chretién de Troyes and the quotation comes from his *Cligès*, 157–8. See Guittone, *Lettere*, 236.

4 It is Peire Rogier and the song is "Senh' en Raymbaut per vezer" ("My lord Raymbaut seeing," *BdT* 356,7). See Guittone, *Lettere*, 236. The references to troubadour texts are given, as is customary, according to the numbering established by Pillet and Carstens in *Bibliographie der Troubadours* (*BdT*).

12 The Blessed Jerome says that virtue does not appear only at sea, or in moments of danger; it also appears at one's bedside when there is danger of illness and when every virtuous person loses the strength of his spirit and the crown of patience and virtue. And it is a great virtue to win where others lose, since he who conquers everyone is stronger than everyone.

13 And therefore, father, I say that he who proves himself best in adversity deserves the most praise. As fire shows the value of gold, hardship shows a man's virtue, and just as fire is apt to refine gold, so is hardship apt to refine man.

14 As Augustine says: "The furnace of hardship burns the wood of vice and purifies the gold of virtue." And for this reason I think that nothing is more to be avoided than quiet consolation, where one loses one's valour, and nothing is more desirable than necessary distress, in which a man attains. For if we are not worthy, we are forced to become worthy, and if we are already worthy, we are forced to improve.

15 As both a bad and a good horse need to be spurred and incited, the same applies to man. Just as a horse acquires vices in laziness, men lose their worth and goodness.

16 Therefore Christian, where Alexander the Younger, says:

"Rest and praise
do not go well together."

17 A certain Provençal writer says:

"By eating well and resting soundly
a man can become evil,
but he who wishes to maintain a good reputation
is charged with much travail;
he must toil here and there,
and must take and give as
time and reason dictate."

18 E però viso m'è, padre, che chi non vale aferma di non valere e chi vale perde valore in agio. E ciò che ten l'omo è al pugnato avere per suo valore: valore non più se pare né mai apparerea, non bisogno apparisse a che tornasse. Ma come se perde in agio, in mesagio s'acquista, ché vile pro', e negrigente vaccio, e scarso largo fa pungente sperone de gran bisogno.

19 Adonque dretto omo, che non soave già ama né dolce, ma valoroso e orrato, seguendo disagio, fuggerà agio, stando a la sentenza del buono Trogil di Troia, che spessamente leggete nel libro vostro, el quale dice che "per pregio avere dovemo più amare travaglio che nullo avere."

20 E voi che donque, padre caro, farete? ché tutta la vita vostra avete fuggito agio e dimandato travaglio, onta perdendo e acquistando pregio: perderete ora nel tempo di coronare, per debilezza di corpo u per viltà de core? "No è vertù cominciare, ma permanere."

21 Certo, padre mio caro, tanto lungamente avete usato travaglio e disusato poso – acciò che lunga usanza torna a natura – , deveria el corpo vostro e l'animo anco tenere disagio ad agio; sì come intendo che già alcuna fece, secondo che Galieno pone, che dal principio suo fue costumata a pascerse de veneno con altra vidanda mesto, e tanto venne da picciula cosa a grande che s'aconciò ad esso, e d'esso el corpo suo notria infine; e forse poi triaca sereali stata veneno.

22 E voi, se dal principio infine ad ora pasciuto in amarezza e in periglio di guerra grande con poco de dolce mesto, dovereste ora pascere e sostenere in propia tribulazione, e, se non pascere, almeno non sentire né dovereste guàire dolere; ché come Tulio dice: "Angustia cotidiana quasi come un callo a dolore face."

23 Mercé, caro padre, mercé de voi stesso, non foco giungete a foco a guisa de misero om, ma acqua, né tribulazione a tribulazione, ma bon conforto; ché sempre è uso di vile e miser omo far d'un danno dui, e del pro' e pregiato tornare l'uno a neuno e prendere di danno pro per forza di cor saggio e bonità valorosa.

24 In sommo gaudio eterno l'alma di Pier Vital tegna Nostro Segnore, se piace Lui, ché valoroso valore e pro' proezza sembra che dimorasse in lui, dicendo:

18 And for this, father, it seems to me that in laziness the unworthy confirm their lack of valour, and the worthy lose their valour. What belongs to us is the fact of having fought to confirm our valour, for it does not appear, nor would it ever appear, if there were no need of it. But just as one loses through comfort, one acquires through discomfort, for the spur of need makes the coward courageous, the negligent diligent, and the stingy generous.

19 So a just man, who loves neither softness nor sweetness but valour and honour, will pursue discomfort and flee from leisure, following the good Troilus of Troy, whom you know well: "If we seek merit, we should love labour more than any other possession."

20 And what, my dear father, will you do then? You spent your whole life fleeing leisure and seeking labour, losing shame and gaining praise. Now, when you are about to be crowned for your efforts, will you lose everything out of bodily weakness and baseness of heart? "There is no virtue in beginning something, but only in persisting."

21 Certainly, my dear father, you have so long been accustomed to labour and unaccustomed to laziness, and since a prolonged habit becomes second nature, your body and spirit should take discomfort as comfort. Galen mentions a similar incident of a woman who, from a very young age, mixed poison with her food, gradually increasing the dose until she grew so accustomed to it that her body fed on it. And at that point the antidote would perhaps have been poison to her.

22 And you, if it is true that you have hitherto fed on bitterness and on danger of war mixed with only scant sweetness, you should now be able to feed on and bear true hardship. Or, if you cannot feed on it, you should at least neither feel it nor be hurt by it, for as Cicero says: "Daily hardship is like a callus to pain."

23 Have mercy on yourself, dear father, do not pour fire on fire, like a wretch, pour water; do not add hardship to hardship, take good advice. Base wretches are in the habit of multiplying their pain, and the courageous and praiseworthy reduce theirs to none, finding profit in harm through the strength of their wise heart and valiant goodness.

24 May Our Lord, if it pleases Him, keep the soul of Peire Vidal in highest eternal joy, for it seems that the greatest valour and courage dwelled in him, when he said:

25 "Con soprasforzato affanno
traggo foco chiaro de fredda neve
e dolce aigua de mare,
...
d'ira benvoglienza
e di piangere gaudio entero
e d'amaro dolce savore,
e sono ardito per paura
e so guadagnare perdendo
e, quando son vinto, vincere altrui."[5]

26 Non perde, no, né disconforta già valoroso om, naturale e prode, avvegna che pò avvenire, ma segue quella parola, la quale Senaca dice: "Non cosa è tanto acerba, ove solaccio non prenda animo bono."

27 No è prod'omo né vigoroso quello che muta come fortuna, or nel monte, or nel valle, e non già mai permane in uno stato; ché fermezza e valore d'animo grande se mostra a quello medesmo esser sempre, avvegna che avvenir pò, come Socrate foe, come si dice.

28 No è vertù, non, quella la quale è sottoposta a podere e a corpo, che, quando podere cade a corpo turba, se turbi; ché vertù d'animo grande congiunta a Quello che no inferma né muta, né infermare né mutare non pò, non muterà.

29 E però parerà ad esta fiata se naturale o inferma è vostra vertù; e se radicata è da Quello, lo quale è non mutabile sommo bono, non muterà; e onni cosa la qual non muta conven che vittoria prenda de tutte mutabile e vane cose.

30 E non solo chi non muta, ma chi più dura in battaglia o in cosa altra, finale è vincitore; unde dice el proverbio: "Chi più dura la vince." Che è, che, duro e forte tanto, che fortezza d'animo grande in continua e saggia operazione non metta a fine bona e vittoria aggia?

---

5 Guittone translates here from Peire Vidal's poem *Pus tornatz sui en Proensa* (*BdT* 364, 37). These lines may well provide instances of moral resilience useful in comforting Orlando, yet what is particularly relevant here is Guittone's admiration for a troubadour like Peire Vidal, famous for his hyperbolic statements and his "folly." Peire Vidal's own treatment of troubadour commonplaces might have provided Guittone with a model for his critique of courtly language in general. See my position in *Guittone d'Arezzo e le maschere del poeta*, 92–3.

25 “With extreme toil
I extract clear fire from cold snow
and sweet water from the sea,
. . .
benevolence from anger
and complete joy from tears
and sweetness from bitterness;
fear makes me courageous
and I can win by losing
and in defeat I defeat the other.”

26 A valiant, healthy, and courageous man does not lose; nor does he ever despair. Come what may, he follows the words of Seneca: “There is nothing so bitter that a good spirit cannot find solace in it.”

27 A man is neither vigorous nor valiant when he changes like the wind, blowing first on the mountain, then in the valley, never remaining in one state. Firmness and strength of spirit appear when one remains constant, come what may, as Socrates apparently did.

28 What depends on power and the body is not a virtue, for when power fails and the body is troubled, it too is troubled. Strength of spirit cannot and will not fall ill or change when it is joined to That Which does not fall ill or change.

29 So this time your virtue will prove itself either ill or healthy, and if it is rooted in Him, who is the immutable highest good, it will not change; and every thing which is immutable will perforce triumph over all things that are mutable and vain.

30 And he who triumphs in the end is not only one who does not change, but one who lasts longer in battle, or in some other endeavour. As, therefore, the proverb says: “He who persists, prevails.” How can a tough, strong person who always wisely uses his great strength of spirit for good ends not gain victory?

31 Levise donque, leve la vertù dell'animo vostro grande, se tutto 'l corpo giace infermo e franto, e 'l poder è voi diserto e tolto, ché voi assai è rimaso, e ricco siete e sano anche ve dico, se vostro animo è sano in sua vertù; e s'el fusse infermo e povero fatto, infermo e povero direa vol, se tutto sano e ricco fuste, come fuste unque.

32 Levisi donque, levi, se sano è, e mostri ad esto punto che valore di valoroso omo vale a tempo di grande bisogno; e gauda, gauda, padre, l'animo vostro!

33 Ché se merciadro più gaude quanto più sente accattatori di sua robba venire, quanto più valoroso e prode omo, amatore de vertù, desideratore di pregio e di vittoria, gaudere e confortare dea, vedendosi da onni parte intorno assiso d'assedio potente, e istretto e assaglito d'assalto grande sovente, fine a quello ch'el crede potere portare, mettendo tutto podere!

34 Provato ha già sovente vostro valore ed è laudato molto, ma non fu mai in punto da prender compiuta laude, ché picciulo misteri fornir è picciulo onore, e grande, grande e bono.

35 Lo Signore Dio, bel padre, da cui onni fortezza, con quale è leggero molto vincer leoni e senza cui perder con agnelli, v'aforzi e amaestri sostenendo e vincendo, come sia maggiormente Lui glorioso e salutevile voi in tutte cose.

31 Let the virtue of your great spirit rise even though your entire body lies ill and broken, and your force is drained from you, for you still have much left. You are also rich and healthy if the virtue of your spirit is healthy. And if your spirit became poor and ill, I would call you poor and ill even if you were completely healthy and rich as you once were.

32 Father, let your spirit arise and rejoice if it is healthy, and now show that a man's valour shows itself in times of great need.

33 If a merchant rejoices more the more buyers he sees for his merchandise, how much more should a worthy and valiant man, a lover of virtue, desirous of praise and victory, rejoice and take comfort when he sees himself surrounded by a powerful siege, hemmed in and attacked, exhausting all of his strength to resist?

34 Your valour has proved itself many times and is highly praised, but it has never been close to earning complete praise, for fulfilling a small task warrants a small honour, while fulfilling a great one warrants a great and good honour.

35 Father, may the Lord God – from whom all strength comes, beside whom it is easy to defeat lions, and without whom it is easy to be defeated by lambs – may the Lord give you strength and teach you to hold on and prevail in whatever way brings greater glory to Him and greater health to you.

Friar Guittone: Moral and Religious Canzoni[1]

1 The texts reproduced here follow the critical edition established by Contini for *Poeti del Duecento* except for the third, "Graziosa e pia," given in the diplomatic version established for the *Concordanze della lingua poetica italiana delle Origini* (*CLPIO*), vol. 1, edited by D'Arco Silvio Avalle. They are reprinted by kind permission of the Istituto della Enciclopedia Italiana Treccani, collana Riccardo Ricciardi Editore.

I[2]

Ora parrà s'eo saverò cantare[3]
e s'eo varrò quanto valer già soglio,
poi che del tutto Amor fuggh' e disvoglio,
e più che cosa mai forte mi spare:
ch'a om tenuto saggio[4] audo contare
che trovare – non sa né valer punto
omo d'Amor non punto;
ma' che digiunto – da vertà mi pare,
se lo pensare – a lo parlare – sembra,
ché 'n tutte parte ove distringe Amore
regge follore – in loco di savere:
donque como valere
pò, né piacer – di guisa alcuna fiore,
poi dal Fattor – d'ogni valor – disembra
e al contrar d'ogni mainer' asembra?

Ma chi cantare vole e valer bene,
in suo legno a nochier Diritto pone
e orrato Saver mette al timone,
Dio fa sua stella, e 'n ver Lausor sua spene:
ché grande onor né gran bene no è stato
acquistato – carnal voglia seguendo,
ma promente valendo

---

2 *Canzone* with *fronte* ABBA and *sirma* symmetrically divisible, except for the last line, and densely interspersed with internal rhymes C(c4)Dd(d5)C(c5)(c5)E, F(f5/4) Gg(g5)F(f5)(f5/4)E, E; *envoy* identical with the *sirma*. Note that in the first stanza only A = C. The text is transmitted by L, V, P, and R and is numbered XXV in Egidi's edition, *Le rime di Guittone d'Arezzo*.

3 The text opens the section in L dedicated to the poems, which immediately follows the letters, and it is the first of the 24 attributed to the converted Guittone. As explained in the introduction, the *canzone*'s strategic position underlines the value of the change in the poet's life, and with its insistent palinodic attitude orients the reading of the following texts as well, both the poems by the friar and the erotic production of the pre-conversion period.

4 It is almost certainly Bernart de Ventadorn who, in his song "Chantar no pot gaire valer" ("He cannot sing or be worthy," *BdT* 70,15), claims that the ability to write poetry depends on the poet's inspiration by love. Luciano Rossi has recently indicated that the polemical target could instead be none other than Guido Guinizzelli. See Guido Guinizzelli, *Rime*, ed. Luciano Rossi.

I

Now it will be evident if I can sing
and if I can be as worthy as I have been
now that I disavow so completely and flee from Love,
that has become more hateful to me than any other thing.
A man many consider to be wise has said
that one cannot write poetry, that one is utterly worthless
when one is not in Love.
Yet, if we think about this,
allowing our minds to follow our words,
it will appear far from the truth,
for everywhere that Love tightens its noose
madness, and not reason, reigns.
Therefore, how can a man be worthy
or agreeable in any way,
if he is so far from the Maker of all worth
and so like His opposite in every way?

But he who wishes to sing and be worthy
must put Justice at the helm of his boat
and honourable Wisdom at the rudder,
taking God as his star, and putting his hope in true Praise.
No one has ever won honour or good
by following carnal desire,
but by being worthy

e astenendo – a vizi' e a peccato;
unde 'l sennato – apparecchiato – ognora
de core tutto e di poder dea stare
d'avanzare – lo suo stato ad onore
no schifando labore:
ché già riccor – non dona altrui posare,
ma 'l fa 'lungiare, – e ben pugnare – onora;
ma tuttavia lo 'ntenda altri a misora.

Voglia in altrui ciascun ciò che 'n sé chere,
non creda pro d'altrui dannaggio trare,
ché pro non può ciò ch'onor tolle dare,
né dà onor cosa u' grazia e amor père;
e grave ciò ch'è preso a disinore
a lausore – dispeso esser poria.
Ma non viver credria
senza falsia – fell'om, ma via maggiore
for'a plusor – giusto di cor – provato:
ché più onta che mort' è da dottare,
e portar – disragion più che dannaggio;
ché bella morte om saggio
dea di coraggio – più che vita amare,
ché non per star, – ma per passare, – onrato
dea credere ciascun d'esser creato.

In vita more, e sempre in morte vive,
omo fellon ch'è di ragion nemico;
credendo venir ricco, ven mendico,
ché non già cupid' om pot' esser dive:
ch'adessa forte più cresce vaghezza
e gravezza – u' più cresce tesoro.
Non manti acquistan l'oro,
ma l'oro loro; – e i più di gentilezza
e di ricchezza – e di bellezza – han danno.
Ma chi ricchezza dispregi' è manente,
e chi gente – dannaggio e pro sostene

and abstaining from vices and sin.
Thus a man of good sense should always be ready
to use all his heart and strength
to advance his state with honour
and not shy away from hard work;
for idleness will not bring wealth,
but rather pushes it away, while fighting brings honour.
Though one should take that the right way.

We should all wish for others what we wish for ourselves;
no one should believe that he can profit from other people's harm,
for what strips us of honour cannot bring advantage,
nor can what is devoid of grace and love bring honour;
and what has been acquired dishonourably
can hardly be used with praise.
But an evil man will never believe
that he can live without being deceitful, and yet far greater
could be proved, by more people, the man who is right at heart:
for shame is more fearful than death,
and being wrong is more fearful than suffering a loss.
A wise man should wholeheartedly love
an honourable death more than life,
for everyone should believe that he has been created
not for present honour, but for the honour he will attain.[5]

An evil man is an enemy to reason;
he dies while alive and always lives as though he were dead.
He becomes a beggar while thinking he will get rich,
for a greedy man can never be rich.
As one's wealth grows
so too do one's greed and worry.
Not many people acquire gold,
it is rather gold that acquires them; and most are hurt
by their own nobility, wealth, and beauty.
Rich is he indeed, however, who despises wealth,
and reacts nobly in both good times and bad;

5 The sense is that man's duty is to pursue honour not for earthly benefits but for the reward of heaven. One could also understand *onrato* as a legacy and moral example to be left behind for future generations.

e dubitanza e spene
e si conten – de poco orrevelmente
e saggiamente – in sé consente – affanno,
segondo vol ragione e' tempi dànno.

Onne cosa fu solo all'om creata,
e l'om no a dormir né a mangiare,
ma solamente a drittura operare,
e fu descrezïon lui però data.
Natura, Dio, ragion scritta e comune,
reprensïon – fuggir, pregio portare
ne comanda; ischifare
vizii, e usar – via de vertù n'empone,
onne cagione – e condizion – remossa.
Ma se legge né Dio no l'emponesse,
né rendesse – qui merto in nulla guisa
né poi l'alm' è divisa,
m'è pur avisa – che ciascun dovesse
quanto potesse – far che stesse – in possa
onni cosa che per ragion è mossa.

Ahi, come vale me poco mostranza!
ché 'gnoranza – non da ben far ne tolle,
quanto talento folle;
e mai ne 'nvolle – a ciò malvagia usanza,
ché più fallanza – è che leanza – astata.
No è 'l mal più che 'l bene a far leggero:
ma' che fero – lo ben tanto ne pare
solo per disusare
e per portar – nel contrar disidero:
u' ben mainero – e volontero – agrata,
usarl' aduce in allegrezza onrata.

in doubt and hope.
Rich is he who is honourably content with little,
who wisely bears pain in silence,
following what reason and the times dictate.

All things were created for man alone;
and man was not created to sleep and eat
but only to behave justly,
and for this he was given intelligence.
Nature, God, philosophy, and common sense
command us to fly from blame
and be deserving of praise; they command us to
avoid vices, and to follow the way of virtue
once every excuse and obstacle have been removed.
But even if neither the law nor God demanded it,
and it were not to give reward either *here* on earth
or when the soul departs,
I would still believe
that every one should strive as much as he can to
let reason be the guide of all things.

Alas, what little use is this knowledge to me!
For it is not ignorance that drives us from doing good
but mad desire.
Indeed, it is rather bad habit that drags us to it,
as disloyalty is craftier than loyalty.
Evil is not easier to perform than good;
and yet the good seems so hard to us,
only because we are out of practice
and so often desire the opposite:
where good is at home and is warmly welcomed,
habit transforms it into an honoured joy.

II[1]

O tu, de nome Amor, guerra de fatto,[2]
segondo i toi cortesi eo villaneggio,
ma segondo ragion cortesia veggio
s'eo blasmo te, o chi tec' ha contratto.
Per che seguo ragion, non lecciaria,
und'ho già mante via
portato in loco di gran ver menzogna
ed in loco d'onor propia vergogna,
in loco di saver rabbi' e follia;
or torno de resia
in dritta ed in verace oppinïone;
e, se mostranza di viva ragione
valer potesse ai guerrer ditti amanti,
credo varraggio lor, ché 'n modi manti
demosterrò la lor condizion rea.

Peggio che guerra, Amor, omo te lauda,
tal perché fort' hailo 'ngegnato tanto
ch'ello te crede dio potente e santo,
e tal però ch'altrui ingegna e frauda.
Lo vil pro', parladore lo nisciente
e lo scarso mettente
e leial lo truiante e 'l folle saggio
dicon che fai, e palese 'l selvaggio;
ma chi ben sente, el contrar vede aperto.
E, se fuss'esso certo,
onta gli è, perché foll'è la cagione,
perché non misur'ha ei né ragione;
e s'ei fusse ch'al ben far non soggiorna,

1 *Canzone* with *fronte* ABBA and *sirma* CcDDEeFFGGE; one *envoy* identical with the *sirma* (CcDDEeFFGGE) and one replicating only its last seven lines (EeFFGGE). The text is transmitted by L, V, and P, where it lacks the first stanza almost entirely. It is numbered XXVIII in Egidi's edition, *Le rime di Guittone d'Arezzo.*

2 The text's refusal of courtly love is a direct polemic against its canonical defence contained in "Cel qui s'irais ni guerrei ab Amor" ("He who raves and fights against Love," *BdT* 10, 15), by the troubadour Aimeric de Peguilhan, but can also be read as a palinode of Guittone's own "Ahi Deo, che dolorosa" ("Ah Lord, the reason for my song"), VII in Egidi's edition and reproduced here with the pre-conversion songs.

II

They call you Love, but war is what you are.
Your followers think I behave rudely,
but reason dictates that it is courtly
to blame you and all those who have dealings with you.
I follow reason, rather than the bad habits
which so often led me
to lies instead of truth,
and to shame itself rather than honour,
to rage and folly in place of wisdom.
And so, I now return from heresy
to the righteous true faith:
and if those warriors called lovers
could be swayed by plain reason,
they would find me very helpful,
as I am adept at showing them the evil of their ways.

Though you are worse than war, Love, one praises you
because you have deceived him so completely
that he believes you are a powerful and holy god;
another praises you so that he can deceive and fool others.
They say you make the ignorant eloquent,
and the stingy generous,
the criminal loyal, the mad wise,
and the close-minded open;
yet the well-informed know the exact opposite.
And even if it were true,
shame on the lover for the cause deprives him
of both sense and proportion.
And even those who dismiss Love but do not dwell in goodness

ma parte Amor, partendo onta li torna,
ché, fallendo ben far, pregio è diserto.

Dicon anche di te, guerra, nescienti
che ben li è troppo, e s'è mal, sì n'è bono;
ciò che non per ragion defender pòno,
ma fai lor sì parer, tant'haili venti.
Ché 'l principio n'è reo: ch'attende e brama
ciò che maggiormente ama;
mangiar, dormir, posar non può, pensando
pur di veder lei che lo stringe amando;
e 'l mezzo è reo, ch'adessa el fa geloso;
afamat' e bramoso
sta manti giorni, e poi pascesi un'ora
u pogo u troppo in angostia e in paura;
e se bon fusse el primo, el mezzo e tutto,
la fine è pur rea: per che, destrutto
principio e mezzo, reo te solo coso.

Peggio che guerra, via reo se' più ch'omo:
ché l'omo perde in te discrezïone
e la razïonale operazione,
per che non poi tra gli animali è omo;
ch'el mesconosce Dio, e crede e chiama
sol dio la donna ch'ama;
con magna gioia el suo strugge, e li pare
ricco conquisto e onorato fare,
consummar sé, che men pote e men vive;
e gire ove receve
morte, talor sembra'i tornar più verde.
Adonque Dio, onor, pro e sé perde;
e, poi perduto ha ciò, perd' ogni amico:
procaccia che? ch'un denaio falso, dico,
chi l'avesse, faria'l forte più dive.

O ver destruggitor, guerra mortale,
nato di quello unde mal tutto vene,
como s'apprende il tuo laccio, e si tene!
Che grave forzo e saver contra i vale?
Ché Sanson decedesti e Salamone;

are still to be shamed for their dismissal,
for where there is no good, there can be no praise.

The ignorant say there is much good in your war,
and that good comes from any evil there might be.
One cannot reasonably defend such an idea,
but you have won them over so thoroughly that they believe it.
The *beginning* of Love's war is evil for the lover awaits
and covets what he loves the most;
he cannot eat, sleep, or rest, for he constantly wonders
how he might see the woman who holds him captive by his love.
The *middle* is evil, for she always makes him jealous.
For many days, he lives in hunger and desire,
then, distressed and fearful, he feeds for one hour
on either too little or too much.
And even if the beginning, the middle, and everything were good,
the *end* is evil; for having destroyed
the beginning and the middle, you alone I pronounce evil.

You are worse than war, much more evil than any man,
for a man loses his discernment
and his rational judgment because of you
that he no longer has what separates him from animals;
for he denies God, and treats
the woman he loves as the only god.
He joyfully destroys his own property, and thinks it
a rich and honourable conquest
to waste all of his possessions, and then, to live so diminished;
and he often seems
to regain vigour by going towards death.
Then he loses God, honour, profit, and his own self;
and afterward, loses all of his friends.
And what does he achieve by this? I think he would be
better off with counterfeit money.

Lethal war, true destroyer,
born from the source of all evil,
it is impossible to break free once one is caught in your trap!
What use are force and wisdom against it?
For you deceived Samson and Solomon;

ma lor non-defensione,
ahi, che grand'onor porge a chi defende!
Donque miri om che reo mal di te scende,
e pensi ben lo valor de la cosa
che gli è tanto amorosa:
ché schifo e conoscente omo dovria
volere desmembrato essere pria;
ch'è però tanto mal per te bailito,
che peggio val che morto om vivo aunito,
e morto onrato mei' ch'en vita posa.

Peggio che guerra, Amor, non t'ho blasmato
perché m'ai' affannato
più ch'altro, o meno messo in tuo van bene:
ch'oltra merto e ragion, quasi for pene,
me desti più ch'a omo altro vivente.
Ma ragion non consente
ch'om laudi el reo perché ben lui n'avegna:
e, quand'eo penso ben, saver m'asegna
che ciò che l'om di te pregia, ben maggio
è, segondo ragione, ont'e dannaggio,
per che te blasmo e pregio ormai neiente.

Canzone mia, tutto che poco vaglia,
demonstrar te travaglia
lo periglioso mal del detto Amore,
e di' che scusa alcun'ha de follore
omo de folleggiare appoderato;
ma quelli è senza scusa assai colpato
che no li tocca guerra e cher battaglia.

but, by comparison, their lack of resistance
gives such great honour to those who resist you!
Man ought therefore to look at the evil that comes from you,
and think well upon the value
of what is so dear to him,
for a cautious and intelligent person would
rather be dismembered first.
You are the cause of so much evil,
because a dishonourable man is worth less alive than dead,
and an honourable man dead is better than one alive.

Love, you are worse than war. I did not blame you
because you made me suffer
more than you did others, or kept me less in your vain graces:
in fact, beyond my worth and beyond reason, and almost painlessly,
you gave me more than to any other living man.
But it is against reason
to praise evil simply because we derive advantages from it;
and, when I think about it, wisdom teaches me
that what we praise in you is in reality
more shameful and damaging.
Therefore I now condemn you without reservation.

I hope that my song may show,
in however small a way,
the dangerous evil of so-called Love,
and declare that folly can be somewhat excused
in a man falling victim to a seizure.
But guilty beyond excuse is the man
who seeks a battle when there is no war.

III[1]

Grasiosa e pia,[2]
virgo dolce Maria,
per mercé ne· 'nvia – a salvamento!

Envia ·ne a bon porto,
vero nostro conforto,
per le cui man' n'è porto – tutto bene;
in la cui pietansa
tutt'è nostra speransa,
che ne· doni allegransa – e tolla pene;
ché, fòr tu dolce aiuto,
chatun fora perduto,
sì come credo, tant'è fallimento.

Adonque, dolce amore,
gioia d'alm' e di core,
di perfetto savore – ed etternale
come noi pò più cosa,
di core stare amorosa,
che servir te, pietosa, – poi sì vale?
Ché ben pò star sicuro,
chi ben t'am' a cor puro,
d'essere pago in tutto el suo talento.

Ahi!, perché sì non piace
acquistar te verace,
come l'aver fallace – d'esto mondo?
Già qual fusse signore
d'ogni terren riccore,

---

1 *Ballad* with stanza aa(a)b[7+4], cc(c)b[7+5], ddX[11], and *refrain* identical to the *fronte* yy(y)X[7+5]. The text is transmitted only by L and is numbered XXXVI in Egidi's edition, *Le rime di Guittone d'Arezzo.* The Italian text reproduced here is the one established for the *Concordanze della lingua poetica italiana delle Origini* (*CLPIO*), vol. 1, edited by D'Arco Silvio Avalle.

2 This is a religious ballad in honour of the Virgin Mary, as is the fragmentary mystical dance "Or vegna alla danza" ("Come now to the dance"), L in Egidi's edition. Texts XXXV, XXXVII, and XXXVIII are also religious ballads, respectively in honour of Jesus, St Dominic, and St Francis.

III

Sweet Virgin Mary,
so gracious and pious,
have mercy and put us on the road to salvation!

Send us to a good haven,
you, our true comfort,
from whom we receive every good.
In whose mercy
lies all our hope
that you give us joy and take away our pains;
for, without your sweet help,
each one of us would be lost:
so great, as I believe, is our trespassing.

Sweet love,
you are a joy to the soul and the heart,
perfect and eternal pleasure.[3]
How then can anything
be more dear to our hearts
than to reap the riches that come from serving you, who are so pious?
For anyone
who truly loves you with a pure heart
is certain to have all of his desires rewarded.

Alas! Why do we find it less pleasing
to win you, who are true,
than to have the false things of this world?
Even if one were lord
of every earthly richness

3 The Italian *savore*, literally "taste," is etymologically connected with *savere*, "knowledge."

no gl'impierrebe core, – tant'è perfondo.
Ma solo è Dio possente
in pagar tutta gente
di tutto sonmo eternal pagamento.

O cor dur e fellone,
mira com' ài ragione
d'onni part' e cagione – in Cristo amare,
ch'Ell' è tuo creatore
e d'el ben ch'ài datore,
e che mortal dolore – volle portare,
per adur ·ce de noia
ala celestial gioia;
e ragion n'ài, ché d'un ben te· dà cento.

Ma sì t'à gran savore,
lass' – om, terren dolciore,
che del tuo criatore – non ti· sovene.
Ma certo poi la morte
troppo ·l comperrai forte,
ché d'ogni dolor sorte – e onni pene
verran sovra te lasso,
e serai vano e casso
del gran dolcior, ch'al bono à Dio convento.

Ai!, per Dio, bona giente,
no più sì malamente
seguiamo ad iscente – nostro danno!
Mettiamo in Dio servire
tutto coral dezire,
ché veggio ad om sofrire – gran tenpo afanno,
sol per ghaudere un'ora.
Ai!, perché non labora
per istar maisempre a sì gran ghaudimento?

Viva e surgente véna,
la qual ben tutto mena,
presiosa reina – celestiale,

his heart would never be filled, so greedy it is.
God alone has the power
to repay every person
with the highest eternal reward.

Oh hard, criminal heart,
consider how you have every reason
and occasion to love Christ,
for He is your creator
and the source of the good you have.
He chose to suffer mortal pain
in order to lead us from torment
to celestial joy.
Heart, you should rightfully love Him, for He repays every good
a hundred times more.

But you miserable man, you find
earthly sweetness so delicious
that you forget your creator.
But after your death you can be sure
that you will pay dearly for your earthly good,
for you will suffer
every pain and every torment
and you will be deprived
of the great sweetness that God has promised to the good.

Oh! Good people, in God's name,
let us no longer pursue
our own destruction with such insistence!
Let us put all our heart's desire
into serving God,
for I see people suffer lengthy torments
just for an hour's pleasure.
Oh! why do they not labour
to maintain their great joy forever?

Living, surging fountain,
which brings every good,
precious celestial queen,

per tua santa mercede
sovra noi provede,
ché forte ciascun sede, – forte male!
Ma tu, che poderosa,
cortese et pietoza
se' tanto, mette in noi consulamento!

watch over us,
with your holy mercy
for everyone thirsts after great evil!
But console us,
you, who are so powerful,
courtly and merciful!

IV[1]

Vegna, – vegna – chi vole giocundare,[2]
e a la danza se tegna.

Vegna, vegna, giocundi e gioi[a] faccia
chi ama Te, da cui sol' onni gioia;
e chi non T'ama, Amor, non aggia faccia
di giocundare in matera de noia.
[S]degna, [s]degna;[3] – non pò che reo portare
chi Te, gioioso, disdegna.

No è mai gioia né solaccio vero
che'n Te amar, Gesù sponso meo caro:
tant' amabel se' tutto e piacentero,
dolc' è Tec' onni dolce e onni amaro.
Tegna, – tegna – lo core in Te amare,
sì che tutt'altro disdegna.

Profet' e santi invitan noi, Amore,
che 'n allegranza Te dovemo amare,
e cantar canti e inni in Tuo lausore
und'onni lauda e onni gloria pare.
Stregna, – stregna – Amor noi sempre fare
ciò che d[e]ritto n'asegna.

O vita vital per cui ëo vivo,
for cui vivendo moro e vivo a morte,
e gaudio per cui gaudo e son gioivo,
for cui gaudendo onni dolor mi sorte,

---

1 *Ballad* with stanza AB, AB (x2x2) Yx8 (x = -egna, Y = -are), and *refrain* identical to the *sirma* [(x2x2) Yx8]. The text is transmitted only by L and is numbered XXXIX in Egidi's edition, *Le rime di Guittone d'Arezzo.*

2 The text is a religious ballad in the form of an invitation to a mystical dance. It might have been written at the behest of the nuns to whom the text refers at line 34. The very same apostrophe to a not-otherwise-identified group of nuns is to be found at line 2 of Letter X, "Ad abadesse e donne religiose" ("To abbesses and religious women"), where Guittone exhorts the addressees to a scrupulous observance of the rule of their order.

3 The correction is suggested by Contini, *Poeti del Duecento,* 230.

IV

If she wants to rejoice, let her come
and keep to the dance.

Let her come, rejoice, and make joy,
the one who loves You, the sole source of every joy.
May those who do not love You, Love,
not rejoice in matters of turmoil.[4]
Let her disdain, if she will; disdain for you, O joyous one,
can only bring evil.

There is never joy or true solace
but in loving You, Jesus, my cherished bridegroom:
you are so completely pleasing and lovely,
that every sweetness and bitterness is sweet with You.
May she keep her heart in loving you,
and disdain all else.

O Love, prophets and saints invite us,
to love You in happiness,
and sing songs and hymns in Your praise
where all praise and glory appear.[5]
May love force us always to do
what justice teaches us.

Life-giving life that I live for,
without which, though alive, I die and live as in death;
joy for which I rejoice and I am joyful,
without which, though rejoicing, I receive all sorts of pain:

4 Except for the true joy of loving God, all other rejoicing comes from "matter of turmoil."

5 That is, find its source.

degna, – degna – la mia alma sponsare
e farlaTe tutta degna.

O vero gaudio del mio spirto, gauda
con tutto piacer di Te l'alma mia,
sì che Tuo viso veggia e Tua voce auda
loco 've gaudio tutto eternal sia.
Regna, – regna – in me sì, che regnare
mi faccia com' giusto regna.

Or venite, venite e giocundate,
sponse del mio Signore e donne mie,
e de tutt'allegrezza v'allegrate,
amando Lui de pur cor ciascun die.
Sdegna, – sdegna – bon cor ciò che non pare
c'al tuo Segnor ben s'avegna.
Tegna, – tegna, chi cher pene, penare,
e a Tua danza non vegna.

consent[6] to marry my soul
and make it worthy of You.

Oh true joy of my spirit, may my soul
rejoice in you with all pleasure,
so that I may see Your face and hear Your voice
in that place where all joy is eternal.
Live in me so that
I may live as the just man lives.

Now come and rejoice,
ladies and brides of my Lord,
and be happy of all happiness,
loving Him every day with a pure heart.
A good heart should disdain what seems
inappropriate to her Lord.
And let her suffer if she wants to be in pain
for she shall not come to Your dance.

6 The subject is *vita vital,* that is, Jesus.

Guittone d'Arezzo: Love Canzoni[1]

1 The texts reproduced here all follow the critical edition established by Contini for *Poeti del Duecento* with the exception of the first one, reproduced in the version established by Michelangelo Picone in the appendix to his "Filologia cinquecentesca," 88–93, reprinted by kind permission of Casalini Libri. The texts from *Poeti del Duecento* are reprinted by kind permission of the Istituto della Enciclopedia Italiana Treccani, collana Riccardo Ricciardi Editore.

I[2]

Se de voi, donna gente,[3]
m'ha preso amor, non è già meraviglia;
ma miracol semiglia
come a ciascun no aia l'anima presa:
che de cosa plagente
saven de virità ch'è nato Amore;
or da voi, che del fiore
del plager d'esto mondo sete appresa,
com pò l'om far defesa?
ché la natura entesa
fo di formare voi co 'l bon pintore
Polocrito[4] fo de la sua pentura;
che cor non pò pensare
né lingua devisare
che cosa in voi potesse esser più bella.
Ahi, Deo, con sì novella
pote a esto mondo dimorar figura
ch'è de sovra natura?
ché ciò che l'om di voi conosce e vede
semiglia per mia fede
mirabel cosa a bon conoscidore.

Quale donque esser deo
poi tale donna intende il meo preghero

---

2 *Canzone* with *fronte* aBbC, aDdC, and *sirma* ccEFggHhFfIiE; *envoy* AbbCcAaDdE. The text is transmitted by L, V, and P, as well as R and other less important manuscripts. It is numbered I in Egidi's edition, *Le rime di Guittone d'Arezzo*. Egidi's text (and Pellegrini's before him) does not include the five lines (here 114–18) transmitted by L and R only, which were either part of a lost stanza or of the first *envoy* that Picone accepts for his critical text.

3 This is the first of Guittone's erotic songs in L, and it only appears to pay homage to his lady. In reality, as Leonardi demonstrates, the text pokes fun from a bourgeois, realistic perspective at the very notion of courtly love. The stereotypical language inherited from the troubadour tradition and revived by the so-called Sicilians is reutilized with ironic intent. Guittone constantly alludes to poems by Sicilian authors and by Giacomo da Lentini in particular. For a thorough analysis of the references and the parodic implications, see Leonardi's "Tradizione e ironia nel primo Guittone," in *Guittone d'Arezzo nel settimo centenario della morte*, 138–48.

4 Polyclitus was a Greek sculptor, rather than a painter.

I

It should come as no surprise that love has captured me
because of you, gentle lady.
The miracle is rather
that not every soul has been taken captive.
Since we truly know that
love is born of what is pleasing.
How can a man protect himself
from you, who encompass in yourself the flower
of the pleasure of the world?
In fact, nature intended
to form you as the good painter
Polyclitus formed his painting;
for the heart cannot think,
nor the tongue explain,
what could be more beautiful in you.
Oh, Lord! how can such a novel image,
which is in fact supernatural,
dwell in this world?
What one knows and sees of you
truly seems to me
something extraordinary even to an expert.

So how should I feel
when such a woman hears my prayers

e mertal volontero
a cento dobbli sempre il meo servire?
Certo miracol ch'eo
non morto son de gioia e de dolzore,
poi como per dolore
pò l'omo per gioia morte sofferire;
   Ma che lo meo guerire
è stato co' schermire,
ver' ciò mettendo tutta mia possanza;
ché quando troppo sentola 'bondare,
mantenente m'acorgo
e con dolor socorgo
quale me credo che magior mi sia:
ché de troppo grassia
guerisce om per se stesso consummare,
e cose molto amare
gueriscon zo ch'e' dolci alcidereno:
de troppo bene è freno
male, e de male troppo, è benenanza.

   Tantosto, donna mia,
com'eo vo' vidi, foi d'amor sorpriso;
né giamai lo meo aviso
altra cosa che voi non devisòe.
E sì m'è bon ch'eo sia
fedele voi, ché 'n me non trovo cosa
ver' ciò contrarïosa,
che l'alma e lo saver deletta ciòe;
   per che tutto me dòe
voi, cui più che meo soe:
meo non son già ch'a far vostro piacere;
che volontero isfareime in persona,
per far cosa di mene
che più vi stesse bene,
che già non m'osa unqu' altro esser a voglia,
c'ubidir vostra voglia;
e s'eo de voi disio cosa alcuna,
sento che savi bona,
e che valor vi rende ed allegranza;

and willingly rewards
my service a hundred times more than it is worth?
It is surely a miracle that I
did not die of both joy and sweetness,
for one can die from joy,
as well as from pain;
but I in fact recovered
because I protected myself
with all my might,
for when I feel too much joy
I immediately fix the situation
with as much pain
as will overpower it.
For the cure for an excess of fat
is to lose weight;
and very bitter things
heal us where sweet ones would kill;
evil is a restraint for too much good,
and good for evil.

The moment I saw you, my lady,
love took me by surprise
and never again were my thoughts
on anything else but you.
And so I consider it right to be
your servant; I find nothing
against it
since it delights both my soul and reason.
Thus I give myself completely
to you, to whom I belong more than to my own self:
I belong to myself only to please you;
for I would willingly undo my own person
to make myself
what pleases you:
for I dare desire nothing more
than to obey your desire;
and, if I desire anything at all from you,
I feel that it is also right by you,
and it increases your worth and happiness.

di tal disïanza
non piaccia Deo che mai possa movère.

Per tutto ciò non servo
né porea mai servir, l'onor né 'l bene,
che per voi fatto m'ène;
ché troppo è segno d'amoroso amore
far lo signor del servo
su' par, ed è ben cosa che non mai
pot'om mertare assai;
donque, como di merto avrò onore?
che, sì como l'Autore[5]
pon c'amistà di core
è voler di concordia e desvolere,
faite voi me che zò volete ch'eo.
Ma bon conforto m'ène
che, con più alto tene
signor suo servo, più li pò valere;
e non pò l'om capere,
sol per servire, en la magion de Deo,
sì como sento e veo;
ma bona fede e gran voglia in più fare
l'agiuta e 'l fa poggiare:
che voglia e fé tal de' fatto valere.

Eo non posso apagare
a dir, donna, de voi l'animo meo;
ché, se m'aiuti Deo,
quanto più dico più talento dire;
none pò dimostrare
la lingua mea com'è vostro lo core:
per poco non ven fore
a direve lo so coral desire.
Acciò ched e' servire
potesse, ed avenire

5 It is very likely Sallust, possibly known to Guittone through St Jerome.

May God will
that I never stray from your love.

All of this does not make me your servant and cannot ever
compensate[7]
the honour and the good
that you do me.
It is a sign of excessive love
for a lord to make the servant
his equal; and it is something that a man
can never fully deserve.
Then how can I be worthy of honour?
The Author states that true friendship
means desiring and not desiring in concord;
then you may do to me what you please
since you and I already want the same thing ...
And I take good comfort
in the fact that the higher a Lord
raises his servant, the greater use he can be;
and as I hear tell, a man cannot enter
the house of God simply by serving;[8]
yet good faith and a strong desire to do more
help and advance him,
for such desire and faith should be worthy of the fact.[9]

I never tire of opening
up my soul to you, my lady,
for, may God help me,
the more I say the more I wish to say.
And my tongue cannot
express how much my heart belongs to you:
in fact, my heart nearly spills out
trying to tell you of its true desire.
And so that I may fully serve you
and increase my favour
with you I wish

7 There is probably an ambiguity in the use of the terms *servire* and *mertare*, both used in both active and passive meanings.

8 The service to the lady is analogous to the service to God.

9 Entering the house of God and entering more into the lady's good graces.

en quale loco più fosse megliore,
vorrea che l'amistà nostra de fatto
ormai donna s'usasse:
che se per me s'osasse
dir, troppo tarda enver' ciò dimorate:
che de fare amistate
certo 'l [troppo] tardar me pare matto,
e comperato accatto
non sa sì bon, como quel ch'è 'n don priso;
e, sì como m'è viso,
endugio a grande ben tolle savore.

[..................
....
.... -ore
.... -ura
....
....
....
................................]
una statov'ho donna a voi sembrante,
che li me sto davante,
sì como l'omo face a la pentura
de Dio in sua figura;
e rendo lei per voi grazi' e onore.

Currado da Sterleto,[6] mea canzone
vo' mando e vo' presento,
che vostro pregio vento
m'ha voi fedele e om de quanto vaglio;
e se non mi travaglio
de vostra or[r]anza dir, quest'è cagione,
che bene en sua ragione
non crederea giamai poter finare:
non de' l'om comenzare
la cosa unde no sia bon fenidore.

---

6 Currado da Sterleto was a very important figure associated with the Emperor Frederick II and his son Manfred and a champion of Ghibelline allegiances. He was very probably the person to whom Guittone referred at line 48 of his letter XVII in verse. On Currado, see Guittone, *Lettere,* 190, and Leonardi, *Canzoniere,* xv.

that our friendship may now
realize its full potential,
and be more concrete.
For if I dare say so,
you are a bit too slow in this regard.
It is madness to delay
joining in friendship
for something bought
does not taste as good as something given;
and I think
delay takes the taste away from what is good.

[....................
....
....
....
....
....
....
.................................]

Lady, in front of me
I keep a statue in your image,
just as one does with a painting
of God in our own image,
and honour and revere it as if it were you.

Corrado from Sterleto,
I present my song to you,
for your praise has won me over
as your faithful servant, for whatever I may be worth.
And if I do not make more effort
in singing your praises, this is because
I do not believe that I could ever be able
to do it as well as your worth deserves:
one should never start
an enterprise that one cannot properly accomplish.

II[1]

Ahi Deo, che dolorosa[2]
ragione aggio de dire,
che per poco partire
non fa meo cor, solo membrando d'ella!
Tant'è fort' e angosciosa,
che certo a gran pena
aggio tanto de lena,
che di bocca for traga la favella;
e tuttavia tant' angosciosamente,
che non mi posso già tanto penare,
ch'un solo motto trare
ne possa inter, parlando in esta via;
ma' che pur dir vorria,
s'unque potesse, el nome e l'efetto
del mal, che sì distretto
m'av'a sé, che posar non posso nente.

Nome ave Amore:
ahi Deo, ch'è falso nomo,
per ingegnare l'omo
che l'efetto di lui cred' amoroso!
Venenoso dolore
pien di tutto spiacere,
forsennato volere,
morte al corpo ed a l'alma lo coso,
ch'è 'l suo diritto nome in veritate.
Ma lo nome d'amor pot'om salvare,
segondo che mi pare:
amore quanto *a morte* vale a dire,
e ben face amortire

---

1 *Canzone* with *fronte* abbC, addC, and *sirma* EFfGgHhE; *envoy* identical to the *sirma* (EFfGgHhE). The text is transmitted by L, V, and P, as well as R and other manuscripts, and is numbered VII in Egidi's edition, *Le rime di Guittone d'Arezzo.*

2 Although the text seems to be somewhat traditional in its treatment of the subject matter, one could argue that, on the one hand, Guittone resorts to the *interpretatio nominis* to revive the classic equation of love and death, but on the other, thanks to the pun, also reveals and underlines the fundamental ambiguity of the language of love lyrics.

II

Ah Lord, the reason for my song
is so painful
that even remembering it
nearly breaks my heart!
It is so cruel and terrifying
that I hardly
have enough breath
to pull the words out of my mouth;
and I am always so terrified to speak
that I cannot bear the pain
necessary to pull out
a single word, unbroken;
and yet, if only I could, I would name the illness
and the effects it has
holding me so tightly
that I cannot rest at all.

Its name is Love,
oh Lord, which is false,
deceiving anyone
who believes that it has a loving effect!
Poisonous pain
full of every unpleasantness,
mad desire;
I call it death to body and soul,
and that is its true name.
Yet I believe that Love's name
can be saved:
love amounts to saying *to death,*[3]
and indeed it extinguishes

3 The original pun relies on the phonic similarity between *amore* (love) and *a morte* (to death).

onor e prode e gioia, ove si tene.
Ahi, com'è morto bene
qual ha, sì come me, in podestate!

Principio de l'efetto
suo, che saver mi tolle
e me fa tutto folle,
smarruto e tracoitato malamente,
per ch'a palese è detto
ca eo son forsennato:
sì son disonorato
e tenuto noioso e dispiacente.
E me e 'l meo in disamore ho, lasso,
e amo solo lei che m'odia a morte;
dolor più ch'altro forte
e tormento crudele e angoscioso,
e spiacer sì noioso
che par mi strugga l'alma, il corpo e 'l core,
sento sì, che 'l tinore
propio non porea dir: perciò me'n lasso.

Amore, perché tanto
se' ver' mene crudele,
già son te sì fedele,
che non faccio altro mai che 'l tuo piacere?
Ché con pietoso pianto
e con umil mercede
ti so' stato a lo piede
ben fa quint'anno a mercé chedere,
adimostrando sempre il dolor meo,
ch'è sì crudele, e la mercé sì umana:
fera no è sì strana
che non fosse divenuta pietosa;
e tu pur d'orgogliosa
mainera se' ver' me sempre restato,
und'eo son disperato
e dico mal, poi ben valer non veo.

Orgoglio e villania
varrea più forse in tene

honour, profit, and joy wherever it takes hold.
Alas, anyone in its power, myself included,
might just as well be dead!

Let me begin with its effect,
depriving me of reason,
making me completely mad,
lost and so terribly unhinged
that everyone says
that I am out of my mind.
I am so dishonoured
and people consider me troublesome and unpleasant.
I disdain myself and all that I have,
and only love the woman who hates me with a passion.
I suffer a pain stronger than any other,
a cruel and terrifying torment,
such a persistent unease
fairly destroying my soul, my body, and my heart.
This is what I feel and can find no appropriate words
to describe it and therefore give up.

Love, why are you
so cruel towards me,
if I am such a faithful servant
that I do nothing but what pleases you?
I have lain at your feet now
for five years, begging for mercy,
in pain, unrequited,
crying pitifully.
This is indeed cruel,
while mercy is so humane:
no wild beast is so savage
that it would not show some pity;
and yet you have always been so scornful towards me
that I am desperate,
and speak poorly,
and I cannot see good prevail.

Pride and villainy
would probably be more successful with you

che pietanza o mercene,
per che voglio oramai di ciò far saggio:
  ché veggio spesse via
per orgoglio atutare
ciò che mercé chiamare
non averea di far mai signoraggio.
  Però crudel villano enemico
seraggio, Amor, sempre ver' te, se vale;
e, se non piggior male
ch'eo sostegno or non posso sostenere,
faraime adispiacere,
mentre ch'eo vivo, quanto più porai:
ch'eo non serò giamai
in alcun modo tuo leale amico.

  O no Amor, ma morte,
quali e quanti dei pro'
d'onore e di pro
hai già partiti e parti a malo engegno!
  Ché gioi' prometti forte,
donando adesso noia;
e se talor dài gioia,
oh, quanto via piggior che noi' la tegno!
  como che venta pei' che perta a gioco
è, segondo ciò pare.
Per ch'io biasmare te deggio e laudare:
biasmar di ciò, che miso al gioco m'hai
ov'ho perduto assai;
e laudar che non mai vincer m'hai dato;
perch'averia locato
lo core in te giocando, e or lo sloco.

  Amor, non me blasmar s'io t'ho blasmato,
ma la tua fellonesca operazione:
ché non ha già ladrone
de che biasmi signor ch'ha lui dannato,
ma da sentirli grato
se merta morte e per un membro è varco;
com'io te de l[o] marco
de lo mal tuo non ho grano un pesato.

than pity and mercy;
and I will now give just such an example,
for I very often see
pride achieve things where
asking for mercy
would never succeed.
For this, Love, I will always be your poor, wretched enemy
if it might serve some purpose.
And since I cannot bear a worse pain than I now bear,
you will be hateful to me
as long as I live,
as much as it is possible,
for I will never again be
a loyal friend to you.

Oh not Love, but death,
how many of the brave
have you deceitfully stripped,
and still strip, of honour!
You promise joy,
bringing only pain instead;
and if you sometimes bring joy,
it is so much worse than pain!
Just as winning at gambling is worse
than losing.
Therefore I blame and praise you:
I blame you for putting me in the game
where I lost much;
and I praise that you never let me win;
because I would have put
my heart in you and now I put it aside.

Love, do not blame me if I blame you,
blame your evil ways:
for a thief has no reason to blame
the lord who condemned him,
but should rather be grateful to lose only a limb
when he rightly deserves death.
So I weigh not one grain
of the grave evil you have done me.

III[1]

Gente noiosa e villana[2]
e malvagia e vil signoria[3]
e giùdici pien' di falsia
e guerra perigliosa e strana[4]
fanno me, lasso, la mia terra odiare
e l'altrui forte amare:
però me departut'ho
d'essa e qua venuto;[5]
e a la fé che 'l maggio spiacimento
che lo meo cor sostene
è quel, quando sovene
mene d'essa, o de cosa
che vi faccia reposa:
tanto forte mi è contra talento.

Certo che ben è ragione
io ne sia noios' e spiacente,
membrar ch'agiato e manente
li è ciascun vile e fellone,
e mesagiato e povero lo bono;
e sì como ciascono
deletta a despregiare
altrui più ch'altro fare;
e como envilia e odio e mal talento
ciascun ver' l'altro ei porta,
e ch'amistà li è morta

---

1 *Canzone* with *fronte* abba e, *sirma* CcddE, ffggE; two *envoys* identical to the *sirma* (CcddE, ffggE). The lines of the *fronte* are a mixture of 8- and 9-syllable lines, while the *sirma* is a mixture of 7- and 11-syllable lines. The text is transmitted by L, V, and R and is numbered XV in Egidi's edition, *Le rime di Guittone d'Arezzo.*

2 Folena already noticed how the text is constructed by means of a hybridization of different genres typical of troubadour lyric, the political *sirventes,* the listing of unpleasantnesses that characterizes the *enueg,* and the erotic song of distance. See Folena, "Pensamento guittoniano."

3 The Ghibellines who were in power in Arezzo.

4 It could be the war of 1259 with Cortona and Florence or the war of 1256 with Guido Guerra.

5 It could be Bologna, or a Guelph city not in Tuscany.

III

Troublesome, uncouth peasants,
evil, corrupt leadership,
deceitful magistrates,
a dangerous foreign war
all make me hate my own country
and love another's.
That is why I left my home
and came here.
And truly the greatest pain that my heart has
is when
I am reminded
of it, or of anything
that is there.
That is how much I loathe it.

There is certainly a reason
why I am troubled and displeased with my homeland.
When I recall that the wealthy are cowardly and evil
while the good are poor and uncomfortable;
and when I recall that people
like nothing
better than to
drag others down.
Everyone bears a grudge
towards someone else;
friendship is dead

e moneta è 'n suo loco;
e com' solazzo e gioco
li è devetato, e preso pesamento.

Membrar noia anche me fae
como bon uso e ragione
n'è partuto e rea condizione
e torto e falsezza li stae;
e che scherani e ladroni e truianti
meglio che mercatanti
li vede om volonteri;
e com' no li ha misteri
om ch'en altrui o 'n sé voglia ragione,
ma chi è lausengeri
e sfacciato parlieri
li ha loco assai, e quello
che mostrar se sa bello
ed è maestro malvagio e volpone.

Donque può l'om ben vedere
che, se me dol tanto membrare,
che lo vedere e 'l toccare
devia più troppo dolere:
per ch'om non pò biasmar lo me' partire;
e, s'altri volme dire:
– Om dia pena portare
per sua parte aiutare – ,
eo dico ch'è vertà, m'essa ragione
e[n] me' part'è perdita:
ch'eo l'ho sempre servita
e, fomi a un sol ponto
mestier, non m'aitò ponto,
ma fomi quasi onni om d'essa fellone.

Parte servir ni amare
d[ev]ia, ni spezïale amico;
ché segnore ni cap'ho, dico,
per cui dovesse restaurare;
ni 'n mia spezialitate a far li aveva,
ni la guerra voleva;

and money has taken its place;
solace and joy
are banished, and pain has become an institution.

It also troubles me to recall
how good manners and reason
have fled, while falsehood
and evil ways remain,
and murderers, thieves, and shysters
are held in higher esteem
than merchants;
and a man seeking justice for himself and others
is quite unwelcome;
only flatterers
and shameless ranters
have a place, or those
with a shiny exterior,
masters of cunning and evil.

Clearly, therefore,
if the mere thought is so painful to me,
the greater the pain would be
were I to embrace my homeland once again.
One cannot blame me for leaving;
and, if someone were to tell me:
– You must even bear suffering
to help your own side –
I say this is true, but no longer holds
for my side:
I have always served my homeland,
and, on the one occasion
when I needed its help, I received none;
in fact, I was treated almost like a traitor.

I must neither serve nor love my side,
nor even friends;
for I have no lord or master
who could restore my fortune.
I was unable to ply my trade there;
I did not want war;

la casa e 'l poder ch'eo
li avea era non meo,
mai lo teneva dal comune in fio
sì, che dal prence en Bare[6]
lo poria a men trovare;
per ch'amo ch'el sia strutto
com' me struggeva al tutto,
sì che nemico non avea più rio.

Estròvi donque, perdendo
onore, prode e plagire,
e rater[r]òmi di gire
ad aquistare gaudendo?
No: stianvi quelli a cui la guerra piace
e prode e bene face;
tutto che, se catono,
com'eo, potesse a bono
partir, piccolo fosse el remanente;
ma l'un perché non pòe
e l'altro perché a ciòe
istar tornali frutto,
biasma el partire en tutto;
ma so che 'l lauda en cor lo conoscente.

Non creda om che paura
aggia me fatto partire
– ché siguro istar e gire
ha più vile ch'eo tra le mura – ,
m'è ciò ch'ho detto con giusta cagione;
e se pace e ragione
li tornasse a durare,
sempre vorria là stare;
ma che ciò sia non veggio, enante creo,
languendo, megliorando
e 'n guerigion sperando,
d'essa consommamento:
per che chi 'l partimento
più avaccio fa, men dann'ha 'l parer meo.

6 The reference is to King Manfred.

the house and the land I
had there were not my own,
I only rented them from the town
for far more than the Prince of Bari
would have asked;
I would therefore be happy to see it ruined
as it so thoroughly ruined me,
leaving me with no greater enemy.

So, should I then stay, losing
honour, profit, and pleasure,
and abstain from going elsewhere
and acquiring things happily?
No: let those who like war stay,
those who profit from it.
If everyone
could really leave,
as I did, there would be precious few left;
but because some cannot
and others stay
because it is to their advantage,
they blame those who leave;
but I know that the wise man praises my departure in his heart.

Do not believe that I left
out of fear
– for there are greater cowards than I
who come and go freely within the city walls –
what I said is correct,
and if peace and reason
returned for good
I would stay there forever;
but I don't see how that could happen; I rather expect
its utter destruction
as I languish here getting better,[7]
hoping for full recovery:
for the sooner one leaves
the less harm is done.

---

7 The sense is that the recovery comes from keeping at a distance from the city.

Solo però la partenza
fumi crudele e noiosa,
che la mia gioia gioiosa
vidila in grande spiagenza,
chè disseme piangendo: – Amore meo,
mal vidi el giorno ch'eo
foi de te pria vogliosa,
poi ch'en sì dolorosa
parte deggio de ciò, lasso, finire,
ch'eo verrò forsennata,
tanto son ben mertata
s'eo non fior guardat'aggio
desnore ni danaggio
a met[t]erme del tutto in tuo piacere. –

Ma, como lei dissi, bene
el meo può pensar gran corrotto,
poi l'amoroso desdotto
de lei longiare mi convene;
ma la ragion che detto aggio di sovra
e lo talento e l'ovra
ch'eo metto in agrandire
me per lei più servire,
me fa ciò fare, e dia portar perdono:
ché già soleva stare
per gran bene aquistare,
lontan om lungiamente
da sua donna piacente,
savendo lui, ed a'llei, forte bono.

Va', mia canzone, ad Arezzo, in Toscana,
a lei ch'aucide e sana
lo meo core sovente,
e di' ch'ora parvente
serà como val ben nostra amistate:
ché castel ben fornito
e non guaire assallito
no è tener pregiato,

But leaving
was cruel and troublesome
only because I saw my joy of joys
in great distress,
for she said to me through her tears: "My love,
woe be the day I
first loved you,
for it has cost me so much,
that I shall go mad.
This is what
I deserve
for never having considered
the dishonour and harm
of putting myself completely at your pleasure."

But, as I told her, she
could also think of my great distress,
since I had to go away from her
amorous delight.
The reasons I've already given,
and the desire and effort
I put into bettering
myself in order to serve her more faithfully,
force me to leave, and she should forgive me.
Moreover, it was customary
for a man to stay away from his beloved
for a long time
in the hopes of a great reward,
and both of them were greatly happy with that.

Song of mine, go to Arezzo, in Tuscany,
go to the lady who keeps on wounding
and healing my heart,
and tell her that it will now be clear
how much our friendship is worth:
for a well-provisioned castle
that is not under attack
deserves less respect

ma quel ch'è asseggiato
e ha de ciò che vol gran necestate.

E anco me di' lei e a ciascuno
meo caro amico e bono
che non dia sofferire
pena del mio partire;
ma de sua rimembranza aggio dolere;
ch'a dannaggio ed a noia
è remesso e a croia
gente e fello paiese;
m'eo son certo 'n cortese,
pregi' aquistando e solazzo ed avere.

than one which is under siege
and in dire straits.[8]

And also tell her and all
of my dear friends
not to suffer
at my absence;
it is I who suffer
at the thought of them:
pining among cruel people
in an evil land.
Whereas I am safe in a courtly company
gaining esteem, comfort, and wealth.

8 The image of a praiseworthy love portrayed as a castle under siege and about to fall is central to understanding the tone of the poem and can be explained in the following manner. If we consider that Guittone's lady had put herself completely at his pleasure (l. 112) and he abandoned her as he did Arezzo, she may now need to fend off suitors attracted by her "reputation." Guittone paradoxically suggests that her good name depends on the fact that she was indeed (and still is) the lover of a very important figure, the one the poet has become through his self-imposed exile.

IV[1]

Ahi lasso, or è stagion de doler tanto[2]
a ciascun om che ben ama Ragione,
ch'eo meraviglio u' trova guerigione,
ca morto no l'ha già corrotto e pianto,
vedendo l'alta Fior[3] sempre granata
e l'onorato antico uso romano[4]
ch'a certo pèr, crudel forte villano,
s'avaccio ella no è ricoverata;
ché l'onorata sua ricca grandezza
e 'l pregio quasi è già tutto perito
e lo valor e 'l poder si desvia.

---

1 *Canzone* with symmetrical *fronte* ABBA, CDDC, and *sirma* EFGgFfE; *envoy* identical to the *sirma* (EFGgFfE); all stanzas are rigorously *capfinidas* (Altezza 15 / Altezza 16, Leone 30 / Leone 31, etc.). The text is transmitted only by L and V and is numbered XIX in Egidi's edition, *Le rime di Guittone d'Arezzo.*

2 The song corresponds to Letter XIV to the Florentines. Margueron, in *Recherches sur Guittone d'Arezzo, sa vie, son époque, sa culture* (19 and following), dates it to the period preceding the conversion, as he does the letter. For the letter as a palinode of song XIX, see Leporatti, "Il 'libro' di Guittone e la *Vita Nova.*" The continuity between song and letter is stressed instead by Cécile Le Lay, "Une lettre pour 'rétracter' après la 'Chanson de Montaperti'?" See also the review by Surdich in *Rassegna della letteratura italiana.* Margueron defines the song as a *sirventes*: an ethical/political text rooted in the most vibrant and contemporary reality with personal names and personal allusions (19–20). The celebrated song mourns the Florentine defeat at Montaperti (4 September 1260), where the Florentine Guelphs were defeated by the Sienese and the German troops of King Manfred called in by the Ghibelline exiles, who thus managed to recapture Florence and exile the Guelphs. It is an "invective against the Ghibellines, who had the audacity to call for German help and find themselves prisoners of their allies. Lambasting the winners whose success weakened Florence, it mixes high political satire with accents of epic poetry, evoking the past grandeur of the city with imperial character, and at the same time sounds the elegiac note of the funeral dirge (*planctus, planh*). Of the *planh* the song retains also the beginning ... and the general intonation, which is not melancholic, but full of passion ... It is a funeral lamentation for the death of the Guelph city ..." (Margueron, *Recherches sur Guittone d'Arezzo, sa vie, son époque, sa culture,* 19–20; my translation). The song is a hybrid of *sirventes* and *planh,* therefore, that substitutes the death of a real person, or the real destruction of a city, with the symbolic death of a city, the symbol of Guelph politics.

3 The Flower is the city of Florence, feminine in the choice of pronouns.

4 The Florentines considered the city to be the rightful heir of ancient Rome (as can be seen in Dante's *Convivio,* I, iii, "la bellissima e famosissima figlia di Roma").

IV

Alas, now is a time of great suffering
for every man who loves Justice;
I wonder where he will find salvation;
I wonder why he has not yet died from the lamentation
of seeing the mighty Flower always bearing fruit
and the honoured ancient Roman custom
headed to certain death. How cruelly miserable
if she is not saved immediately:
for her powerful, honoured greatness
and praise have almost completely vanished,
and valour and power are losing their way.

Oh lasso, or quale dia
fu mai tanto crudel dannaggio audito?
Deo, com'hailo sofrito,
deritto pèra e torto entri 'n altezza?

Altezza tanta êlla sfiorata Fiore
fo, mentre ver' se stessa era leale,
che ritenëa modo imperïale,
acquistando per suo alto valore
provinci' e terre, press'o lunge, mante;
e sembrava che far volesse impero
sì como Roma già fece, e leggero
li era, c'alcun no i potea star avante.
E ciò li stava ben certo a ragione,
ché non se ne penava per pro tanto,
como per ritener giustizi' e poso;
e poi folli amoroso
de fare ciò, si trasse avante tanto,
ch'al mondo no ha canto
u' non sonasse il pregio del Leone.

Leone, lasso, or no è, ch'eo li veo
tratto l'onghie e li denti e lo valore,
e 'l gran lignaggio suo mort'a dolore,
ed en crudel pregio[n] mis'a gran reo,
E ciò li ha fatto chi? Quelli che sono
de la schiatta gentil sua[5] stratti e nati,
che fun per lui cresciuti e avanzati
sovra tutti altri, e collocati a bono;
e per la grande altezza ove li mise
ennantîr sì, che 'l piagâr quasi a morte;[6]
ma Deo di guerigion feceli dono,
ed el fe' lor perdono;[7]
e anche el refedier poi, ma fu forte

5 The Ghibelline party.

6 A reference to the exiling of the Guelphs with the help of Emperor Frederick II in 1248.

7 The return of the Guelphs two years later and the peace of 1251.

Alas, have the likes of such devastating
harm ever been heard before?
God, how can you allow
justice to die and injustice to rise?

The withered Flower had such great power
while she was loyal to herself,
for she acted imperiously,
acquiring many provinces and lands, near and far,
through her great valour.
She seemed to want to build an empire
as Rome had once done; and it seemed
easy, for no one could rival her.
And quite rightly so,
for she cared less about empire
than she did about justice and tranquillity.
And she was so enamoured of her righteous action
that she gained great ground,
for there is nowhere in the world
where the Lion's praises went unsung.

Alas, she is a Lion no more, for I see
her claws and teeth and valour pulled from her,
and her great families painfully killed,
and so unjustly imprisoned.
And who has done this to her? Those who
descend from her noble ancestry,
whom she raised up and favoured
above all others, and whom she placed in positions of power;
and because of their great height,
they became so proud that they nearly killed her;
yet God's gift healed her
and she pardoned them.
And they wounded her again, but she was strong,

e perdonò lor morte:[8]
or hanno lui e soie membre conquise.

Conquis'è l'alto Comun fiorentino,
e col senese in tal modo ha cangiato,[9]
che tutta l'onta e 'l danno che dato
li ha sempre, como sa ciascun latino,
li rende, e i tolle il pro e l'onor tutto:
ché Montalcino av'abattuto a forza,
Montepulciano miso en sua forza,
e de Maremma ha la cervia e 'l frutto;[10]
Sangimignan, Pog[g]iboniz' e Colle
e Volterra e 'l paiese a suo tene;
e la campana,[11] le 'nsegne e li arnesi
e li onor tutti presi
ave con ciò che seco avea di bene.
E tutto ciò li avene
per quella schiatta che più ch'altra è folle.[12]

Foll'è chi fugge il suo prode e cher danno,
e l'onor suo fa che vergogna i torna,
e di bona libertà, ove soggiorna
a gran piacer, s'aduce a suo gran danno
sotto signoria fella e malvagia,
e suo signor fa suo grand'enemico.
A voi che siete ora in Fiorenza dico,
che ciò ch'è divenuto, par, v'adagia;
e poi che li Alamanni in casa avete,
servite'i bene, e faitevo mostrare
le spade lor, con che v'han fesso i visi,
padri e figliuoli aucisi;
e piacemi che lor dobiate dare,

8 An allusion to the Ghibellines' alliance with Manfred resulting in their exile of 1258.
9 At the time, Siena was Ghibelline.
10 The deer and the fruit were a symbolic tribute of submission from the Maremma region.
11 The war bell, the "Martinella."
12 The Uberti family and those who contributed to the Ghibelline victory.

and spared them death.
Now they have conquered her and her dominions.

The powerful Florentine Commune has now been defeated,
thus switching places with Siena
and reaping all the shame and damage that it had
once meted out to her;
and all Florence's profit and honour are taken:
Montalcino has been defeated,
Montepulciano has been subdued,
and the stag and tributes from the Maremma belong to Siena.
San Gimignano, Poggibonsi, Colle,
Volterra and its land are all Siena's;
and the bell, the banners and arms,
the spoils of war are all stripped,
along with everything of value.
And all of this occurs
because of that one mad, mad dynasty.

Anyone who flees his own profit and seeks his own damage
is quite mad;
so too if he turns his honour to shame,
and agreeably lets himself be led
from the great freedom he enjoys
towards harmful, evil servitude,
turning his own worst enemy into his master.
To those who are now in Florence, I can only say
that you seem pleased by what has befallen you;
and now that the Germans are in your own house,
you must serve them well, and ask them to show you
those very swords they used to mark your faces,
and kill your fathers and sons.
I am pleased that you must pay them

perch'ebber en ciò fare
fatica assai, de vostre gran monete.

Monete mante e gran gioi' presentate
ai Conti e a li Uberti[13] e alli altri tutti
ch'a tanto grande onor v'hano condutti,
che miso v'hano Sena in podestate;
Pistoia e Colle e Volterra fanno ora
guardar vostre castella a loro spese;
e 'l Conte Rosso[14] ha Maremma e 'l paiese,
Montalcin sta sigur senza le mura;
de Ripafratta temor ha 'l pisano,
e 'l perogin che 'l lago[15] no i tolliate,
e Roma vol con voi far compagnia.
Onor e segnoria
adunque par e che ben tutto abbiate;
ciò che desïavate
potete far, cioè re del toscano.

Baron lombardi e romani e pugliesi
e toschi e romagnuoli e marchigiani,
Fiorenza, fior che sempre rinovella,
a sua corte v'apella,
che fare vol de sé rei dei Toscani,
dapoi che li Alamani
ave conquisi per forza e i Senesi.

13 The Guidi counts and the Uberti, who were the leaders of the Ghibelline party.
14 Aldobrandino of the Counts of Soana, now Sovana.
15 It is Lake Trasimeno.

a lot of your money, for they worked
very hard to do what they did to you.

Offer a lot of money and many jewels
to the Conti and the Uberti and to all those
who led you to such honour,
and put you under Siena's command.
Pistoia and Colle and Volterra now protect
your castles at their own expense;
the Red Count holds Maremma and its land;
Montalcino is safe without walls;
Pisa fears Ripafratta;
Perugia fears that you will take its lake
and Rome wants to make a pact with you.
So it seems that you
have gained all honour and lordship.
You have achieved your aim,
which was to become master of all Tuscany.

Lombard barons, Romans, Apulians,
Tuscans, Romagnoli, and Marchigiani:
Florence, the perennial flower,
calls you at her court,
because she wants to become queen of the Tuscans,
now that her strength
has defeated the Germans and Siena too.

Guittone d'Arezzo: Teachings on Love[1]

1 In the absence of a trustworthy critical edition of Guittone's corpus, the Italian text is the one established for the *Concordanze della lingua poetica italiana delle origini* (*CLPIO*), vol. 1, edited by D'Arco Silvio Avalle. It is reprinted by kind permission of the Istituto della Enciclopedia Italiana Treccani, collana Riccardo Ricciardi Editore. The English translation often refers to the reading of the text previously supplied by D'Arco Silvio Avalle in his *Ai luoghi di delizia pieni*. The translation also takes into consideration the readings offered by Pellegrini and Egidi in their respective editions: *Le Rime di Fra Guittone d'Arezzo: Volume primo (versi d'amore)* and *Le rime di Guittone d'Arezzo*. The cycle of 24 sonnets is preserved in its entirety only by the Vatican codex (V), where it occupies the series of texts starting at n. 406 and ending at n. 429, folios 119r up to 121r. The first ten sonnets are transmitted also by the Laurentian codex (L) from 362 (f. 136v) to 371 (f. 137v), while sonnets 9 through 24 are transmitted by the Magliabechiano (M) (f. 4r–f. 5v) as well.

Sonetto I[1]

Me piacie dire com'io sento d'amore
a pro di quelli che meno sanno di mene.
Secondo ciò che pone alchuno atore,[2]
amore uno disidero d'animo ène,

disiderando d'essere tenetore
dela cosa che più piace ·li bene;
lo quale piaciere ad esso è criatore
e cosa c'a sua guida lo· ritene.

Pemsero[3] l'avanza e lo· crescie e rinova
e va ·llo sempre im sua rasgione fermando
e fa ·lli fare e dire ciò che vole prova.

Savere lo· va, com' più può, menzonando,
natura il· tène e non vole già che mova,
per cosa alchuna, delo suo dimando.

---

1 Sonnet: ABAB ABAB CDC DCD.

2 The author mentioned must be identified with Andreas Capellanus.

3 "Thinking" here is to be considered the obsessive form usually associated with the phenomenology of love.

Sonnet I

I would like to give my opinion about love
for the benefit of those who know less than I do.
According to what a certain author affirms
love is a desire of the soul

longing to be in possession of
the object that pleases it the most;
such pleasure is both what creates love
and what love keeps as its own guide.

Thinking moves it forward, increases it, and renews it
and keeps it fixed on its object[4]
making it do and say what requires proof.[5]

Reason tries to hinder it as much as it can;[6]
Nature holds it and does not want to swerve
from its requests for any other thing.[7]

4 The object is probably the external object of the love's desire, i.e., the woman. Understanding *rasgione* as "reason," the line should read: "And keeps it always convinced of its reason, its legitimacy, its own right to be."

5 The idea here is that love is forced by the obsessive thinking about the desired object to give proof of its own existence through both deeds and words. The true nature of love is not, therefore, only a mental disposition, but rather a codified set of behaviours, and the treatise will in fact demonstrate what these are.

6 Although the overall meaning of the line is clear, i.e., "rationality tries as hard as it can to counter the rising sway of love on the mind," the word *menzamando* is not. If one could read *men sonando*, "playing it less," with *sonare* used in a similar way as in the last sonnet (see XXIV, 8), the sentence would probably be clearer.

7 No other object of desire can take the place of the beloved (but the word "thing" here and elsewhere has a very materialistic undertone) once love has taken power over the mind.

Sonetto II[1]

Esto amore nonn- è tutti comunale
perché nom sono d'una comprensione,
ché tal è che non mai di ciò li· chale,
e tale che 'm sua chura altro nom pone.

E ciertto sono ched adiviene ch'è tale-
-fiata che l'omo ama e tale che non-e;
e tale ama tale non dé, ttai ch'uguale
sumiglieranno di sua condizione.

Dureza, briga, contrado acidente
adimorare l'ommo fa senza amore:
amore fa core vago e core vertente

or amare or no, e d'uno tinore
istare due; ch'uno ama e l'altr' en nente,
reo acident'è, in quale nonn- è fatore.

1 Sonnet: ABAB ABAB CDC DCD.

Sonnet II

This love is not common to all
for not everyone has the same disposition;
in fact there are those who never care about it
and those who care for nothing else.

And I am sure that some times
a man loves, and some times not;
and some times he loves people he should not,
those who are in circumstances similar to his.[2]

Hardship, strife, adversity
make a man live without love:
love makes both yearning and inconstant hearts

love some times and some times not, and makes of one condition
two;[3] the fact that one loves and the other not at all
is an unfortunate circumstance for which love is not responsible.

2 These lines (7 and 8) are difficult to interpret, and the word *condizione* refers either to a social or perhaps a psychological state. If one were to read "e tale ama tale non de' tai ch'uguale sumiglieranno di sua condizione," the impediment would have to do with social disparity, and the translation would be "and he loves someone not of those from a similar social condition."

3 The phrase "e d'uno tinore istare due" (and of one condition two) is not completely clear. I take it to mean that, since hard external circumstances may prevent a person from following his natural inclinations, the disposition will result in two separate, opposite behaviours.

Sonetto III[1]

È sua natura e suo podere d'amore
ciertto assai meravilgliosa cosa;
ché lo poder è tale, c'altro valore
nonn- à loco ver' llui ove il bene posa;

e sua natura fa il conoscidore
disconosciente e dà laida risposa,
e 'l molto leale falsso e draditore,
e 'l presciato diviene villana cosa.[2]

E fa tutto il contrado bene doblamente,
e gioia e dolo mesclatamente rende,
e' nom poria già dire quanto sovente.

Ora eo nom sono per dire ciò che ne· sciende:
ma pur lo modo solo sempriciemente
como poi facc', a chi d'amore se· 'nprende.[3]

---

1 Sonnet: ABAB ABAB CDC DCD.

2 These lines (5–8) are an almost literal translation from Aimeric de Peguilhan, "Cel qui s'irais ni guerrei ab Amor" ("He who raves and fights against Love," *BdT* 10, 15). The converted Guittone uses them again with an evident palinodic intent in song XXVII, "O tu, de nome Amor, guerra de fatto" ("They call you Love, but war is what you are").

3 Here the author makes it explicit that the purpose of the treatise is not of a speculative nature but rather a didactic one. As I state in the introduction, I propose to consider it mock-didactic (see pages 19–20).

Sonnet III

The nature and power of love is
quite a wonderful thing indeed;
for it has such power that when it takes root
there is no place for any other force,

and its nature makes the wise
unwise and foul-mouthed,
and the most loyal false and treacherous,
and what is praiseworthy becomes shabby.

And it does everything and its opposite;
I could hardly say how often
it mixes together joy and sorrow.

Now, it is not my purpose to say what derives from this:
rather in simple terms to say how
those taken by love must behave.

Sonetto IV[1]

Lo modo del'amante essere dia
tale c', avantiché scovra il suo coragio,
facca che conto dela donna sia,
overo d'omo alchuno di suo lengnagio,

che, 'n casgione di partire lui compangnia,
possa presso di lei tenere usagio,
e che, per lui, a llei ritratto sia,
quand'ello face alchuno bono vassalagio.

Ed ello peni sì far ·llo sovente
che quelli od altro possa assai ritrare
avanti lei di llui presgio valente;

poi c'aconcio avesse sì suo afare,
mostri ·li bene com'è suo benevolgliente
e miri se 'n vista lei piacie o dispare.

1 Sonnet: ABAB ABAB CDC DCD.

Sonnet IV

The way of the lover should be such
that, before he reveals his feelings,
he makes himself acquainted with the lady,
or at least with someone in her family

who, by being part of her entourage,
has free access to her,
and through whom she can be apprised,
of all his worthy exploits.

And he should strive to do so frequently
so that one friend or another may often report
on his valiant worth to the lady;

and once he has arranged his business in this manner
he should show her how devoted he is to her
and judge his welcome from how she looks.

Sonetto V[1]

Perché diverssi causi sono, convene
usare ver' ciò diverssa operazone;
ché, se le· piacie, alegro stare vole bene
e pur penare, com' più piacca a ragione:

e, se le· spare, pur con cheré' merzene
e co· mostrare tormento im sua fazone,
faciendo ciò c'a llei piaciere pertene,
dimorar en lei amare tutta stagione.

Sovra qualunque d'esti causi rengna,
procieda sì com'io gli· ò divisato,
ed intorno di ciò quello che sa vengna;

ché per me no li· può esser ·ce mostrato,
im sì piciola partte, ongnumque imsengna:
im fare e 'n dire sia da sé assennato.

1 Sonnet: ABAB ABAB CDC DCD.

Sonnet V

Since every situation is a different case, one must
go about things in different ways;
for if he is welcome, he should be merry
and also strive to please her, as reason demands;

and if he is not welcome, then by pleading mercy
and showing his tormented face,
and doing things that might please her,
he should persist at all times in his affection.

In whichever of these situations he finds himself
he should proceed as I have taught him
and do what he has learned;

for I cannot teach him here
each and every thing in great detail:
he must be wise in actions and words.

Sonetto VI[1]

Ma eo non mi· credo già c'alchuno amante
si· possa dela sua donna dolere,
ca, 'n tutto il meno, no sia sì benestante
che 'n vista alchuna mostra ·li benvolere;[2]

e ciò che chere, farebe il similgliante,
se ·l si· potesse fare com bello parere.
Or, se "non" dicie, e fa di "sì" sembiante,
deve ·la l'omo però falssa tenere?

Non ciertto già, s'è donna di buono presgio,
che dicie "no," perché non vol mostrare
c'agia talento, poi no nd' à podere;

ché senza frutto avere non vole dispresgio:
sembiante fa perché degia sperare
che donare vole, se temppo e' sa cherére.

1 Sonnet: ABAB ABAB CDB CDB.
2 The lady, with her countenance, will almost always in some way acknowledge and encourage the suitor's persistence.

Sonnet VI

But I do not think that any lover
can really complain that his lady
is not well-enough disposed
to look kindly upon him;

for she would do what he desires,
if she could do it without being blamed.
Now, if she says "no," but seems to be saying "yes,"
should she be considered false?

Certainly not, if she is a woman of good reputation
who says "no" because she does not want to show
that she has desires, which she cannot afford to show,

as she does not want to be blamed for nothing;
she appears interested so that he hopes
she will grant her gifts, if he waits for the right time.

Sonetto VII[1]

Ora dirà l'ommo già che lo podere
ciaschuna donna à bene, poiché le· piacie,[2]
e puote bene stare tanto il piaciere
che vero dicie, tanto che fallacie;[3]

c'à poca volglia e gran senno, 'n vedere,
nom pò poder e fare ciò che comfacie;
e, s'à gran volglia e piccolo savere,
loco e podere assai vede veracie.

Dumque, chi ama peni a valere tanto,
che 'n ubrianza metta lo savere
e cresca volglia, se di lei vole vanto.

Per la gran forza di merzé cherére
la volontà di ciò li· dona manto,
ché contra ciò nom pò pianza tenere.

---

1 Sonnet: ABAB ABAB CAC ACA.

2 There is some ambiguity in the sentence "poiche le· piacie," since it can be understood to imply that women are whimsical but also that they enjoy the kind of power that they have over men.

3 In other words, she can either accept the courtship (and thus acknowledge her desires) or pretend that she does not, even if in reality she is pleased by it and there is always hope for the persistent lover.

Sonnet VII

It will now be said that every woman
has the power, once it suits her,
(and it may very well please her)
to tell the truth as well as to lie.

A woman who seems to have little desire and great perspicacity
cannot permit and do what is necessary;
and, if she has great desire and little judgment,
she clearly sees to the occasion and possibility.

Therefore he who loves should strive to be so worthy
that she puts good sense out of her mind
and gives way to desire, if he wants to obtain her.

Pleading for mercy can be such a powerful tool
in stoking her desire
that her chastity cannot hold out against it.

Sonetto VIII[1]

Or torno a dire che l'amante àve a fare,
dapoich'è per sembianti assai provato.
Entendere dia c'a llei possa parllare
in alchuno loco palese o cielato.

Prenda loco, se può far dimandare;
senòn, dimandi casgione d'altro lato;
ca, per ingiengno e per forza, mostrare
vole la donna che vengn' a tale mercato.

E, s'è cielato in loco ov' e' l'econta,
basci ed abracci e, se comsentimento
le· vede alchuno, prenda ciò che più monta.

Ma, se nom pò di sé fare parlamento,
parlli per tale che sia privata e conta
e sia sua pare, se· vuole, di valimento.[2]

---

1 Sonnet: ABAB ABAB CDC DCD.
2 The choice of *valimento* (worth) also introduces ambiguity regarding the morality of both the middlewoman and the lady.

Sonnet VIII

I now resume saying what the lover must do
after he has been sufficiently assured by her looks.
He should find a way to talk to her
in some public or private place.

He should make an appointment, if she can be reached;
otherwise, he should ask for an occasion of a different kind,
for it is only through deceit and violence
that a woman will show that she is amenable.[3]

And if the meeting place is private,
he should kiss and embrace her, and if he sees
that she acquiesces, he should take what matters most.

But if he can't talk to her in person,
he should talk through an experienced and trustworthy lady
who is necessarily her equal in worth.

3 Literally, "she agrees to such a transaction."

Sonetto IX[1]

Or- -ché dirà, overo -ché farà dire,
dapoic'avene ched à loco e stasgione,
s'è magio, o pare, o minore di podere
la donna, se· vuole guardi per rasgione;

e quale ell'è di loco e di savere
e quale d'atto e quale di condizione:
perché diverssa via si· vuole tenere
colà dov'à diverssa operazione.

Ché tale vole minacca e tale prieghera
e tale cortese dire e tale vilano
e tale parola umile e tale fera;

è tale che dire c'om fortte ama ·l', è sano,
e tale che nonn- è buona, e fa ·si altera
e fa 'l suo core ver' del'amante strano.

1 Sonnet: ABAB ABAB CDC DCD; v. 1: -ire instead of -ere.

Sonnet IX

As soon as he communicates with her, directly or indirectly,
and he has found both the right place and time,
he must carefully consider
the lady's social status, whether it be higher, equal, or lower,

and what she is like in terms of condition and good sense
and also in terms of behaviour and rank;
for a different strategy must be adopted
for each different task.

Some women want threats, and others prayers;
some want courteous words, and others vulgar speech;
some want humble words and others proud ones;

there are some who enjoy being told how much they are loved
while others do not and they become disdainful,
hardening their hearts to the lover.

Sonetto X[1]

Ed en ciaschuna vol ·si conto e sagio
ciaschuno causo guardando, come e quando:
ma le più volte essere cortese e sagio
e' se· vuole propiamente cominzando.

E più ver' dela donna ched è magio,
che versso dela pare diritto usando:
versso dela pare vuol -e' tale usagio,
che vèro dela minore volglia -e' comando.

"Qual è pare, qual è magio, qual è minore?"
mi· pò l'ommo dire; ed io rispondo bene:
"Quella che 'n convenente altro è magiore,

è sovra, sovramagio; quella ch'ène
en altro par, è 'n ciò magiore, forzore;
e quella ch'è minore, pare, simile vene."

---

1 Sonnet: ABAB ABAB CDC DCD.

Sonnet X

One must have information and experience of each woman;[2]
one must consider the time and place of each situation;
yet, most often, the best way to start things off
is by being courteous and wise.

One must behave with the utmost consideration
towards a lady of higher rank than towards an equal.
Towards an equal, one should behave in the same manner,
since one must command only those who are inferior.[3]

"Which one is an equal, which one is superior, and which inferior?"
one might ask me; and I would answer thus:
"The lady who is, in other more serious circumstances, superior,

is far superior; she who is an equal
in other things, is in this case superior to and stronger than him;
and she who is inferior, it seems, becomes an equal."

---

2 The Italian words *conto e sagio* (familiar and wise) could also be taken as adjectives referring to the lover, instead of nouns as I have done here.

3 The idea is that unless the woman is of a lower social condition, she always has to be treated as a superior.

Sonetto XI[1]

Dica, o dire facca, a lei che sormagio ène,
che '· sembiante benevol e pietoso,
che 'l piaciente piaciere che 'n viso tène,
e 'l gran bellore del suo stato amoroso,

e 'l presgio fino c'al suo valore convene,
il dire e 'l fare di llei sì agrazioso,
e tutto ciò che donna àve di bene,
che 'n lei trova ommo che di natura è uso,

la· fa piaciere sì dolzemente, ch'ello
è llei coralemente fedele, quanto
è solo per ubidire ciò che l'è bello.

E che merito di ciò vuole solo tanto,
che lei piacca che suo, senza rubello,
sia mentre viv' e à ·l meritato manto.

1 Sonnet: ABAB ABAB CDC DCD; v. 8: -uso instead of -oso.

Sonnet XI

He should tell a very highly placed lady, directly or through an intermediary,
that her benevolent and merciful countenance,
the pleasant beauty she holds in her face,
and the splendour of her loveliness,

and the high praise appropriate to her worth,
her very graceful words and deeds,
and every noble thing that a lady has
(which is said to be her natural disposition)

make her so sweetly pleasing that he
puts his whole heart into serving her, since
he is there exclusively to do her bidding.

And as a recompense, he only wants
her to allow him to be hers, faithfully,
for as long as he lives and is deserving.[2]

2 With different punctuation, the line could be translated "and (with allowing him to be her servant) she has already recompensed him a lot."

Sonetto XII[1]

Ver' la magio si · vuole quasi tenere
simile modo, sì como laudare,
e tanto dire e fare, e' mantenere
sape di bene, ver' di ciaschuno afare.

E, tanto è grazioso il suo piaciere,
che suo fedele, com' più lei possa amare,
e' vuole sempre essere del corppo e del podere,
se vuole dire, com'io dissi, o dir fare.

E, poi che s'è sì llei tutto donato,
piacca di servire, lei tanto pietosa,
che lle· doni, sua graza e suo buono grato,

almenoché 'n dire ed in sembrare gioiosa,
li· siano resi, sì ben· è sovramertato,
e pachi sì che mai nom brama cosa.

1 Sonnet: ABAB ABAB CDC DCD.

Sonnet XII

One must praise a superior lady
to almost the same degree,
and continually say and do all the good
that one can in every situation.

And so gracious is her beauty,
that in order to love her more,
he will forever want to be her faithful servant, in body and spirit;
thus he must say, as I have said, directly or through an intermediary.

And after one has given himself to her so completely,
she should mercifully accept his service
and at least in words and her happy looks,

grant her gifts, grace, and gratitude
(so greatly has he deserved them),
so that he feel rewarded and desire nothing else.[2]

---

2 The last two lines of the text have created many interpretive problems for all previous editors, and Avalle does not even report them in his edition. The translation departs somewhat from the lesson given by *CLPIO* and is closer to Pellegrini's (and Egidi's) reading.

Sonetto XIII[1]

E llei ched è sì pari, com'agio detto,
dé l'omo ciertto reverenza fare,
c'ommo nom pò, secondo il mio intelletto,
versso d'alchuna troppo umiliare

per condure l'om bene suo diletto:
ch'umiltà fa core umile fare
e lauda le· fa prendere buono rispetto
e tolle ·le di laida risponsione fare.

Dumque umilemente laudando lei facca
dire, overo dica, quanto può più bene,
com'è suo tutto im fare ciò ke llei piacca.

E, pregando per Deo e per merzene,
ritengna ·lo basciando imfra sua bracca,
ché 'n ciò è tutta sua volglia e sua spene.

1 Sonnet: ABAB ABAB CDC DCD.

Sonnet XIII

To an equal, as I already said,
he should clearly pay homage
for, as far as I can see, no man can ever
lower himself too far with a lady

as he moves in on his pleasure:
for humility makes the heart humble,
and praise makes her respectful
and forbids her to react basely.

Therefore, with humble praise he should let her
know, or tell her directly, as best he can,
that his only desire is to do her bidding.

And he should pray, in the name of God and mercy,
that she hold him in her arms and kiss him,
since it is here where all his desire and hope lie.

Sonetto XIV[1]

Modo ci· è anke d'altra condizione,
la quale tengn' -ommo bene perffettamente:
ciò è savere sì dire, che la casgione
possa avere da dire altro parvente;

ché, se tutto la donna àve rasgione
e volglia di tener ·llo a benevolente,
si· vergongna dir "ssì," se la quistione
l'è posta, per lo propio convenente.

Donna vole sempre "non" dire e "sì" fare;
ché "sì" fare vole che sia conosciente,
e vuole d'altra partte dimostrare

che del pemsiero del'omo sacca nente,
e, tutto ciò che fa ver' quello afare,[2]
enfingiere di no far ·llo ad isciente.

1 Sonnet: ABAB ABAB CBC BCB.

2 The "business" here has evident sexual implications.

Sonnet XIV

A man can perfectly well take
quite a different tack altogether:
talking in such a way that his intention
takes on a different appearance from his words;

for even if a lady has good reasons
and she wishes to keep the man in her good graces,
her reputation prevents her from assenting
to an open request.

A woman always says "no" when she means "yes"
because she wants the man to know what she means
and at the same time she wants to seem

unaware of what the man is thinking;
and she pretends to be unconscious of everything
that she does pertaining to such business.

Sonetto XV[1]

Similemente vole c'omo si· 'mfingia
di non vedere, e vegia ongni su' stato,
e vole che sia sagio, per che provegia
e senta suo volere e suo pemsato;

e di tale modo si· conduca e regia
e chegia suo volere sì colorato,
che casgione possa avere che nom s'avegia,
né sacca di venire in tale lato.

Ché per ferm' è ciò ch'io dissi dissovra:[2]
che la donna per forza e per inganno
vole mostrare che vengn' a tale ovra.[3]

Dumque procaccia quelli talora suo danno,
che fa opera lei che si pù scovra,
ché, vergongnando, poi te' ·llo in afanno.

1 Sonnet: ABAB ABAB CDC DCD; v. 1: -ingia instead of -egia.
2 The "before" is sonnet VIII, ll 7–8, where the same concept is expressed.
3 See sonnet XIV, l. 13, for the meaning of the word "business," here more precisely "work, operation."

Sonnet XV

Similarly, she wants the man to pretend
not to see, when in reality he sees her every mood.
And she wants him to be wise so that he can predict
and understand her every desire and thought

and conduct and control himself in a certain way,
and ask for what he wants in such a disguised way[4]
so that she has every reason not to see
where she is headed.

What I said earlier is well known:
a woman wants to show that she is led to love
through violence and deceit.

Therefore, if one tries to make her come out in the open
he may cause his own downfall
for, as she feels ashamed, she makes him suffer.[5]

4 The adjective used actually means "coloured," which has a clear reference to the rhetorical colours.

5 Basically, she keeps him waiting.

Sonetto XVI[1]

In che modo pò l'omo sì dire e fare
como mestere in tale cosa fae?
S'è conto sì c'a llei possa parlare
(che vale più, com' più conto le· stae),

dirà c'alchuna volta e' vuole mostrare
cosa che llei conoscie e sae,
ch'è laida sì che troppo le· dispare;
c'amendare ne· porà, se voràe.

E, se dicie: "Di' ·ll' ora!," el li· può dire
ch'è cosa a dimostrare rimotamente,
s'ella nom se· ne· vole disabellire.

La donna poi se· pemssa, e 'l fatto sente;
e, se per altra guisa e' dé avenire,
però li· avene acioché lgli· è piagiente.

1 Sonnet: ABAB ABAB CDC DCD.

Sonnet XVI

How can a man say and do
what is necessary to reach his ends?
If he is close enough with her to be able to speak to her
(and the closer he is the better)

he will tell her that he sometimes wants to show her
something that she knows and is also aware of,
something so ugly that she would abhor it,
but that, were she willing, he could correct.

And if she says: "Say it now!," he could tell her
that it must be done in secret
if she doesn't want to damage her reputation.

The lady then thinks it over, and sees his intentions;
and if it should come to pass in some other way,
it does so because it pleases her.

Sonetto XVII[1]

Ki nonn- è conto dé fare altro viagio;
ma, chi per alchuno modo essere pòne,
facca che sia, sì farà come sagio:
ché pur può fa' ·llo, se bene mette ·si a cione.

Ché, se l'omo daprima è llei salvagio,
en opo più salvaticheza pone,
se, vergongnando, parlla ·li d'oltragio;
per che tard' à di llei bene sua rasgione.

Ma, s'elgli è conto in oso e 'n dire e 'n fare,
ed ella in ascoltare e 'n consentire,
ed ànno più asgio a fare ciaschuno afare,

siché grave li· può gioia fallire:
ma tuttavia sì volglio -eo dimostrare
modo altr' a quello, s' a ciò non sa venire.

1 Sonnet: ABAB ABAB CDC DCD.

Sonnet XVII

One who is not close should take a different road,
yet if he has any chance of coming closer
it is wise of him to do his best:
for it is possible if one tries one's hardest.

In fact, if the lady does not at first know the man,
she will treat him with much more hostility,
for fear of shame, telling him she is outraged;
and it will therefore take him longer to reach his goal.

But if he is close, daring in words and in deeds,[2]
and she used to listening and agreeing
it will be easier for both to do business

and they will hardly fail to have joy:
nevertheless, I want to show yet
another approach, if this one does not work for him.

2 With different punctuation and taking *conto* to mean here "skilled," Avalle reads: "But if he is skilled in the use of dealing (with such issues)."

Sonetto XVIII[1]

Quando la donna à 'n oste o 'n altro lato
marito o padre o suo procano parente,
facca l'amante come lì sia stato;
poi torni e mandi lei dire inmantenente:

"Madonna, cotale uommo si· è tornato
a chui tale, vostr' amico, uno convenente
impose che diciesse a voi in cielato:
sì ·l vi· vorebe dire, se v'è piaciente."

S'ella s'avede, dicie: "Est' è saciente,
ché 'l messo non vole sacca il volere c' àe
ed io posso mostrare nom sacca nente;

se far llo· degia, or n' ò matera asae."
Se nom s'avede, almeno loco comsente
ove lei parlle; e forsse pì gli· fae.

1 Sonnet: ABAB ABAB BCB CBC.

Sonnet XVIII

When the lady's husband, or father or close relative,
is serving in war or somewhere else,
the lover should pretend that he has been there,
and upon his return, he should immediately have someone tell her:

"Milady, So & So has just returned
and a close friend of yours entrusted him
with a secret for you
that he wishes to tell you, if it please you."

If she understands, she will say: "This fellow is clever
for he doesn't want the messenger to know what his plans are,
and I can pretend that I don't know anything:

if I ever wanted to do it, now is the time."
If she does not understand, she will at least agree
to meet him, and perhaps let him do even more.

Sonetto XIX[1]

Anche si· può la donna inamicare[2]
di donna ed uommo che suo conto sia,
e tanto di piaciere déa ·li fare,
che volontieri in servire lui si· dia:

e dapoi ciò, sarà degno mostrare
quello che lo core suo vole e disia,
e, quanto saverà melglio, pregare
come di ciò atato essere voria.

E, se la donna, o l'ommo che sia, vole bene,
a compimento adesso il fato tengno:
ché, s' a convento a ciò ch' e' vuole non vene,

sì la· conduca a loco per ingiengno;
c'a convent' od a forza pur convene
fare ciò che vò· l'amante fò· ritengno.

1 Sonnet: ABAB ABAB CDC DCD.

2 The subject of the sentence in Italian would seem to be the woman, but it must actually be the lover.

Sonnet XIX

He could also befriend the lady
through a woman or a man who knows the beloved,
and he should do this person so many favours
that she or he will be willing to perform services for him:

and afterward he should explain
what his heart desires
and explain as best he can
how he would like to be helped in the matter.

And if the woman or man agrees
I consider the deed now accomplished.
For if the lady does not willingly arrive at what he wants,

let her be led there by deceit:
so that willingly or by force she agrees to do
what the lover wants, without reserve.

Sonetto XX[1]

Me pare avere bene dimostrata via
che, chi la· sa compiutamente usare,
che per necisità quasi la· dia
chui dura assai coralemente d'amare.

Ma d'essa come l'omo vò· la balia
e com' e' l'agia, nom si· pena guare
se no la partte; e saccio ch'è restia,
e com poco procaccio d'aquistare.

Come dé tal omo donna concherére,
che se· dovria maisempre blasmare
quella che l'acolgliesse in suo piaciere?

Molto vale uommo c'a donna possa stare
a difensione, poi c'omo be· lla· rechere
e li· fa ciò c'op' è ver' quello afare.

---

1 Sonnet: ABAB ABAB CBC BCB.

Sonnet XX

I believe I have already shown those
who have long been loving passionately
a guaranteed way to win a lady,
if they are only able to follow it correctly.

But when a man gets control over her,
he has almost nothing more to worry about,
only she does. And I understand that she is reluctant
and without much to gain.[2]

How can a man conquer a woman
who would constantly blame herself
if she were to welcome him in her pleasures?

The worthiest man is one who defends a woman's
reputation even after he courts her
and does everything he must in the matter.

2 The *come* in both lines could also be read as "how," and the word *parte* can be taken as a noun ("part," referring to the beloved) or as a form of the verb *partire*, here meaning "to separate." An alternative translation of the quatrain would be the following: "But in what way he wants control over her, / and how he gets it, is of no concern / unless he later abandons her. And this is why she is reluctant / and has little profit to gain."

Sonetto XXI[1]

Com prego e com merzé e com servire
e com pietanza e con umilitate
e con essere piagiente im fare e 'n dire
ver' llei e ver' ciaschuno di sua amistate,

e ver' ciaschuna cosa, ond' avenire
possa im buono presgio dele gienti orate,
la· condurà per forza im suo piaciere,
ché contra ciò nom pò avere potestate.

Ma è tal ora che la donna ama di volglia,[2]
vedendo l'ommo di sé bene disioso:
sì si· comfortta e ver' di llui s'orgolglia.

Alora val bene ver' llei far ·ssi orgolglioso
e demostrare che del'amore si· tolglia,
e di melgliore di lei far ·ssi amoroso.

---

1 Sonnet: ABAB ABAB CDC DCD.

2 It is a situation in which the lady wants to play with the lover and make him jealous, a case that, as the next tercet makes clear, calls for counterattack.

Sonnet XXI

With prayers, mercy, and service,
with piety and with humility,
by being pleasant in deeds and words
towards her and to everyone in her circle of friends

and to everything that may raise
her prestige among respectable people,
he will necessarily lead her to do his pleasure,
for she has no power against any of this.

At times, though, when a woman loves willingly,
seeing that the man desires her so ardently,
she takes up courage and becomes hostile.

On such occasions it is best to return her pride
and show that one can fall out of love
and find someone better to love.

Sonetto XXII[1]

Al dire e al dire fare e al cherére
si· vuole guardare loco e stasgione
e lo stato di llei, siché 'l volere,
c'à buono, possa fare buona rasgione:

ché nonn-asgio talora fa sostenere
cosa c'altri à di fare volglia e casgione,
ed asgio le· fa fare ciò che 'n calere
nonn- averia per nulla condizione.

Loco se· vole, dove avenevol sia
a llui di dire, a llei d'ascoltare,
e stasgione quando sta fori compangnia,

e lo suo stato alegro, e 'l suo pemsare
è churocioso, perché fatto sia
per suo marito alchuno noioso afare.[2]

---

1 Sonnet: ABAB ABAB CDC DCD.

2 If she is upset with her husband the lover's chances are increased. Notice the married status of the lady, a commonplace of the ideal love in the troubadour tradition.

Sonnet XXII

As for talking, and letting her know and asking,
one must consider the place, the proper time,
and her condition so that her good will
will yield good results:

since unease sometimes makes one refuse
what one wishes and has occasion to do,
and ease makes her do what she would
not at all care to do.

It is important to find a place
where he is comfortable talking and she listening
and a time when she is by herself

and in a happy state, except for
the negative thoughts occasioned
by some of her husband's troublesome business.

Sonetto XXIII[1]

E' vuole esere l'ommo soferente bene
ver' tutta noia che di ciò gli· avengna;
e, quanto più la donna orgolglio tène,
più umile fare la sua parola e dengna:

e grande prometitore star llo· convene,
e fare che l'omo a bon cieladore lo· tengna
e largo ver' lla donna ov'è sua spene
e 'n arme avanzatore dela sua imsengna.

E' li· convene bene essere conosciente
del volere dela donna e di che fare,
dica sempre, ed in che punto èd im parvente;

e, se nom sa per sé, dé comsilgliare
con omo, che sia di ciò bene saciente,
ed anche a quello che dett'agio, mirare.

---

1 Sonnet: ABAB ABAB CDC DCD.

Sonnet XXIII

And the man must be patient
with any trouble that might come from this,
and the prouder the woman is
the humbler and worthier his words should be,

and he ought to promise much
and have people think him a discreet person
and a generous one towards the lady he hopes for,
and a bearer of her standard in combat.

And he ought to know
what the lady wants: both what she always
says he should do, and what she seems to make evident;[2]

and if he does not know this himself, he should ask for advice
from someone who is knowledgeable in such matters,
and he should also consider what I have said.

2 These two lines (10–11) are particularly convoluted and hard to understand in the original.

Sonetto XXIV[1]

Sempre poria l'ommo dire 'n esta partte,
trovando assai che diciere di bono,
en tante guise dipartit' e spartte
le partti d'essa e le condizioni sono;

però da ciò misi, faccio dispartte
con quello c'ò detto; avengnaché ciaschuno
me· piacie che 'n ciò prenda ingiengno ed artte
e vegia avanti più ch'eo no li· sòno.

Trach'eo sò poco ed ò piciolo aiuto,
loco ed asgio di dire tanto affare,
sò che lo detto meo nonn- à compiuto;

ma tuttavia però non mi· dispare:
pur esere nom porà c'alchuno aiuto
non doni altrui, che n'ostari' il penare.

---

1 Sonnet: ABAB ABAB CDC DCD; v. 6: -uno instead of -ono.

Sonnet XXIV

One could continue talking about this subject,
writing poems that say many interesting things,
for it is so complex, and the elements that compose it
are so numerous and variegated.

Therefore I now step aside from my subject matter
and leave what I have said, for it pleases me that
everyone may learn the tricks and the skill of this business
and see beyond what I actually say.

Since I know little and have little means
and placc and time here to exhaust such business
I know that my poetical work is not finished;

nevertheless I am not dissatisfied
for it cannot but help
someone, and in doing so, relieve his suffering.

Friar Guittone: Cycles on Vices and Virtues[1]

1 The sonnets are presented here according to the text established for the *Concordanze della lingua poetica italiana delle origini* (*CLPIO*), vol. 1, ed. D'Arco Silvio Avalle. They are reprinted by kind permission of the Istituto della Enciclopedia Italiana Treccani, collana Riccardo Ricciardi Editore. The English translation also takes into consideration the readings offered by Egidi in his edition, *Le rime di Guittone d'Arezzo.* Only L transmits the following sonnets starting at n. 225 and ending at n. 252, folios 118v–122r.

Sonetto I[1]

Nesciensia, e ppiù sciensia carnale
e secular, di mal tutt'è cagione;
ché, conoscendo ·l chiaro, null'ama male,
ni mette in che no ama operassione.

Ma charnal sciensa ai soi mostra, sol vale
in carne procurar delettassione.
Superbi, avari e van'! Simil e tale
loro scensa in mond' amar mostra ragione;

e carne o mondo amar, è propia véna;
unde malisia tutta e visio appare
ch'a periglio e a morte el secul mena.

E quanto sciens' è tal maggi' e più chiar è,
maggio nel detto amor voglia fa piena;
e quanto piena più, più fa mal trare.

1 Sonnet: ABAB ABAB CDC DCD.

Sonnet I

Ignorance, and even more carnal and worldly
knowledge are the source of all evil;
for no one who knows what the truth is loves evil,
nor does one do what one does not like.

But carnal knowledge shows its disciples that all that matters is
taking pleasure in the flesh.
Proud, greedy, and vain people! Such knowledge of theirs
shows them it is only reasonable to love the world,

and loving the flesh or the world is an appropriate inclination;[2]
from this stems all the malice and the vice
that leads the world to danger and death.

And the more such knowledge is great and clear,
the greater it increases the desire for such kind of love,
and the greater the desire, the more it leads to evil.

2 The Italian *véna* literally means "seam, vein," as in "coal seam" or "gold vein."

Sonetto II[1]

Superbia, tu sse' capo di peccato;[2]
per te pecca chi pecca in mod' alcono;
visii tutt'altri inforsi e cresci 'n stato,
vertù onne distruggi in onni bono.

Visio de diavol se' propio provato,
e tutti toi spesial' figli soi sono.
Tu solo contra Dio senpr' ài pugnato,
e, ch'Ello ti· sostegna, io non ragiono;

ma funde e funderàe te-i e i toi tutti,
con' diavol, padre vostro, in mal tutto,
e in ciel e in terra àve· li strutti.

Mort' à' 'l mondo, montand' onni corrutto;
montati affiggie, lor temor' desdutti:
e catun quazi in fin ruina strutto.

1 Sonnet: ABAB ABAB CDC DCD.
2 The text revolves around Lucifer's sin of pride, the arrogance that caused his downfall.

Sonnet II

Pride, you are the head of sin:
whoever sins in any way, sins because of you;
you strengthen and increase all other vices,
you destroy every virtue in every good person.

It is clear as day that you are the devil's own vice,
and all of your sons are his own special ones.
You alone have always fought against God,
and I do not believe that He tolerates you,

rather He casts, and will cast, you and all your kin,
as He did the devil, your father, down in hell,[3]
and has them destroyed both in heaven and on earth.

You have killed the world by exalting every type of sinner:
once their fears are allayed, he torments those he has raised;
and everyone falls almost to ultimate ruin.[4]

---

3 The original formulation is *mal tutto*, i.e., "all evil."

4 The verb "raise" refers to people who are raised in both power and pride. The pronoun "he" refers to the devil. The idea is that pride makes you lift yourself above others, but the text is not completely clear. "Everyone" stands for "each proud person."

Sonetto III[1]

Avarisia, tu meriti affanno
de pluzor parte; e molt' angosci' à 'n core,
ove più prende te, con più tradanno;
ché dentro voiti, u' pió enpi di fore.[2]

Ricchesse senpre in te pover-on fanno:
legne a ffoco son, montando ardore;
non mai soggiorno ei toi giorn' e nott' ànno
in acquisto, in guardia od in timore.[3]

Religiosi fai propietari,
sonmoniachi chierchi e baratteri,
baron' rattor', chavaler' uzurieri,

ladrone et fel ciascun nel su' misteri,
d'amici e di fratel' grand' aversari,
e ttener fai quazi Iddio denieri.

---

1 Sonnet: ABAB ABAB CDD DCD.

2 The soul is emptied.

3 The avaricious are restless trying to acquire more, guarding and fearing to lose what they already have.

Sonnet III

Avarice, you deserve to suffer
for many reasons, and the more the heart takes you in,
the greater is its anguish, the greater the damage;
for you hollow the inside as you bolster the outside.

With you, riches always make a man poor;
they are wood on the fire, feeding the flame;
day and night, your disciples have no peace
in acquiring, in guarding, and in fearing to lose.

You turn religious men into landowners,
clerics into simoniacs and barrators,
barons into robbers, knights into usurers,

each one is light-fingered and dishonest in his profession;
you make enemies of friends and brothers,
and you transform coins into a God.

Sonetto IV[1]

Lussuria, tu di saggi' -om matto fai,
adultro cherco, e vil serv' -om signore,
e tutto 'l secul quazi a male trai;
pió de visio altro e pió d'altr'ài vigore.

Corpo 'nfermi, invegli, poder isfai
e tolli pregio e bon d'onni valore.
Spesiale in cherch' e 'n donna, ove restai,
affogha in onta onni lor bene et more.

Ai!, che mercato ontozo e matto avizo,
Dio e ssé dare e coss' onni sua bona
per parva e brutta gioi, mést' a ttormento!

Ai!, che valente e coronato prizo
vincer te, e spesial gioven persona;
e cche ontoza, om saggio esser vénto!

1 Sonnet: ABAB ABAB CDE CDE.

Sonnet IV

Lust, you turn wise men into mad men,
clerics into adulterers, lords into slaves,
and lead more people to evil
than any other vice, and you are stronger than the others.

You make the body sick and old, you undo strength
and devalue all worth and good.
And when you dwell in priests and women,
every good drowns in shame and dies.

Ah! What shameful commerce, what a mad decision
to give away God and oneself and one's every goodness
for such an evil, ugly joy mixed with torment.

Ah! What a worthy and noble prize
for the young in particular to defeat you,
and what a shame for the wise to be defeated.

Sonetto V[1]

Invidia, tu nemicha a catun se' -e,
e ai toi più, che li· consunmi in dogla;
Dio e ssé perde e tutti, hom, boni in tee,
ché d'onni bon nemicha in llui pon vogla.

Catuno tuo prova malvagio sée,
poi odia bono, e llui, se può, s'orgogla;
onni vertù altrui lui visio èe,
e riccore a ppovertà lo· spogla.

L'altrui lucie l'acciecha e onor onta;
triaca è llui veneno e 'l bene male:
odia bon' tutti e grandi, e essi lui.

E quanto ben pió crescie, in mal pió monta:
a ccui sa bon visio retener tale,
tegna ·lo fermo, e ben mostri ·si altrui.

1 Sonnet: ABAB ABAB CDE CDE.

Sonnet V

Envy, you are an enemy to everyone
and more so to your own kind, whom you consume with pain;
through you, men lose God, themselves, and all goodness
for you instil a desire that is the enemy to every good.

Everyone of your kind proves himself evil,
for he hates good people, and is prideful with them when he can.
Every virtue in others is a vice to him,
and their wealth impoverishes him.[2]

Other people's light blinds him, and their honour shames him;
a medicine is poison to him, and good is evil:
he hates all who are good and great, and they hate him.[3]

And the more goodness grows, the more he gains in evil:
let him who manages to restrain such vice
keep it under control, and then show himself to others.[4]

---

2 The line means that the envious person considers himself in poverty as soon as he starts comparing his wealth with another person's.
3 Virtuous people in fact end up rightfully hating the envious person, as he is evil.
4 Since envy has to do with seeing, the envious person who can restrain such vice should legitimately pose as an example.

Sonetto VI[1]

Visio di gola, tu brutto e ontozo[2]
quazi sor tutti, fòr quel di luxura.
Onta fai 'n dir fare far noiozo,[3]
poder desfai 'n ispendi oltra mizura.

Corpo turbi, infermi e fai gravozo,
anima in tee danni, ché fa' · i rancura;[4]
e chi 'n opra di te è poderozo
indanno contra visii altrui lavura.

Lussura inde e vanitate molta
crii nel mondo cierto e cupidessa,
che fa rattori e uzurieri in colta.

E ppió ontoza e grave è tua gravessa,
ché laida è troppo la cagione e stolta;
ché men d'uncia 'n palato è tua dolcessa.[5]

---

1 Sonnet: ABAB ABAB CDC DCD.

2 The Italian *gola* means "throat," which is also one of the places where language is articulated.

3 The glutton speaks in outrageous ways, and every activity becomes for him an annoying task, i.e., he also becomes slothful.

4 Gluttony also eventually leads to wrath, which in turn will curse and damn the glutton's soul.

5 Namely, it amounts to nothing.

Sonnet VI

Gluttony, you are an uglier and shameful vice,
more than any but lust.
You make speech shameful and action painful,
you weaken strength through boundless spending.

You pervert the body, making it sick and heavy,
you condemn the soul that follows you by angering it,
and those who derive their strength from your handiwork
work in vain against the vices of others.

It is certainly you, therefore, who create lust
and much vanity in the world, and greed,
which binds thieves and usurers.

And your seriousness is all the more shameful and heavy
for your excuse is too ugly and stupid;
for your sweetness weighs less than an ounce on the tongue.

Sonetto VII[1]

Tu visio, accidia, a ccui ben fastidioso,
operar è nemico, e tt' è valore
pigrisia, negrigensia e miser poso;
lentessa e tarditate ài 'n amore.

O poltron visio vil, mizer, noioso,
e fastidioso a' bbon' tutti tuttore,
tu nelo stato d'ognon se' odioso,
peccato e danni porgi e dizinore;

corpo 'nfermi, occidi, poder estrai,
onor, amor scacci, visii accogli;
giac' e mangi omo, unde besti' una ·l fai.

Vivi in te son soppellit' i folli,
perigliozo e ontozo a tutti stai,
ma pur a' ccherchi e a' signor' più tolli.

1 Sonnet: ABAB ABAB CDC DCD; v. 10: -ogli.

Sonnet VII

Sloth, you are a vice to whom good is tedious,
and activity is an enemy; you value
laziness, negligence, and miserable rest;
you love slowness and delay.

Oh lazy vile vice, miserable, irritating,
annoying at all times to all good people.
You are hateful to everyone's condition,
you bring sin and damage and dishonour.

You weaken and kill the body, you drain its force,
and chase away honour and love and welcome vices;
a man lies and eats, and you turn him into a beast.[2]

Fools are buried alive in you;
you are dangerous and shameful to all,
but are especially harmful to clerics and lords.

---

2 Reading *giac' e mangi omo* with *CLPIO,* the subject of the sentence remains "sloth," and the text would read "you lay and eat up a man."

Sonetto VIII[1]

Ira, pessimo visio, acciecha mente,
incende e turba om dentr' e di fore,
morde e ppiagha el su' [...] primeramente,[2]
ed enn- altro poi stende el suo furore.[3]

Onne visio in essa è ppió possente;
quale pió val, non val enn- ella fiore,
per che nel tenpo suo è ppió saccente
chi più tacent' è e meno operadore.[4]

Ché, chi la· segue, Dio e ssé li· tolle,
vicin' tutti e amici, e · l fa noiozo,
ed onni bona parte el· dezaccolle,

ché carcare non può -om legno spinozo;
e 'l pió saccente è con ella folle,
e qual è maggio, maggio el· fa ontozo.

1 Sonnet: ABAB ABAB CDC DCD.
2 The missing word probably has to be integrated with *cor*, as in Egidi's edition.
3 Other people or other parts of the body.
4 Namely, he who bites his tongue and can restrain himself.

Sonnet VIII

Wrath is the worst vice: it blinds the mind,
enflames and rattles a man inside and out;
at first, it bites and wounds his [...],
and then it extends its fury to others.

With it every vice is more powerful,
and the worthiest person becomes worthless,
for when it is in command, it is wiser
to be more silent and less industrious.

Its followers are deprived of God and of themselves,
of all their neighbours and friends, and they become troublesome,
and unwelcome to all good company,

as one cannot carry thorny wood.
Wrath makes the wisest man mad
and it puts the mighty to mighty shame.

Sonetto IX[1]

Gloria vana, tu furtivamente
di vertù tutte d'om tolli onni merto;
tu venen dolce e malatia piagente,
laccio mortal di bell'ésca coverto,

tu fai vincendo om esser perdente
de quanto ello procaccia, a te dezerto;
tra i seculari ontisci omo valente,
e fai noiozi di piacenti certo.

Se tutto opera degna om fa d'onore,
non déa chieder honor, né però far · la,
ma in onor de bon solo e dd'amore

di quello, che dà grasia in operar · la.[2]
E, ss'a bon chieder pregio è dezinore,
onta quanta a malvagio è bon stimar ·la?[3]

1 Sonnet: ABAB ABAB CDC DCD.

2 The real goal of a worthy action should be the good and the love of good for itself, which is its own reward.

3 Namely, to consider good what is actually shameful.

Sonnet IX

Vain glory, you stealthily
take away all the merit of a man's virtues;
you are a sweet poison and a pleasant illness,
a deadly trap with enticing bait.

By forsaking him, you make a winning man
lose what he has gained;
among secular people you shame a valiant man
and make pleasant people troublesome indeed.

Even if a man does anything at all praiseworthy,
he should not ask for praise, nor should he be driven by it
but only in honour of the good and for the love

of that which is its own reward.
And if it is dishonourable to ask for praise for doing good,
what greater shame is it for the evil man to consider it good?

Sonetto X[1]

D'animo fievilessa e codardia,
visio dannoso troppo e dizorrato
se gola e carne tenta a villania,
od alcun altro, altro à -dessa hon conculcato.

E ssì, se ccoza, qual aspra lui sia,
el· punge, e' chade et ffa che-vol peccato:
demoni e visii tutti àn segnoria
del tutto d'esso, e sservo è llor provato.

Unde vile è viapiò che fango o sterco,
poi conculcano lui visii e demòni.
O!, quanti alteri son, d'esti vil' servi!

Piò che di bassi trovamo, se cerco;[2]
ma, quanto è maggio tal più, sè ragioni[3]
servo piò vil de' servi e de' conservi.[4]

1 Sonnet: ABAB ABAB CDE CDE.

2 The meaning of line 12 is: "on closer inspection, we find more cowards among proud than among humble people."

3 The reference here is to the social hierarchy.

4 The coservants are the companions in slavery.

Sonnet X

Cowardice, faintness of heart,
is too dangerous and dishonourable a vice.
When gluttony or flesh or something else tempts us to act basely,
cowardice has already brought us down.

So, if a man is stung by anything, no matter how bad,
he falls and does sin's bidding;
demons and all vices command him
completely, and he becomes a slave to them.

He becomes viler than mud or dung
for he is brought down by vices and demons.
Oh how many proud people are among these vile servants!

Many more than the humble, I think we'll find.
And the higher a coward is, he should consider himself
a viler servant than the servants and their coservants.

Sonetto XI[1]

Non-giustizia, ciò è falsessa e torto,
de visio non sol part'è già, ma tutto:
ov'à podere, ogni diritto è morto,
onni leggie, onni ordo, onni uzo è strutto,

per leggie sua propio talento è pporto.
Guai a bbass' -om, che llui avant' è addutto![2]
E guai, sorguai, a cchi più n'à conforto
ed a chi · l ten sortutto in guai corrotto![3]

Onn' è bon giustisia, che ddéa rendendo
a dDio, a ssé ed al suo prossim' -omo;[4]
e, ccon' v'è onni bono, è · vi onne merto.

E ssì tort' onne male è, ritenendo
rapendo e dando ove non déa; e como
è male tutto, onni mal merta certo.

1 Sonnet: ABAB ABAB CDE CDE; v. 8: -otto instead of -utto.

2 It is the situation of the poor man brought before an unjust justice.

3 These are particularly convoluted lines, which are nevertheless a clear accusation of the judge, corrupted and troubled, who enforces an unjust justice and of the individual who benefits from it, who hopes to get out of trouble by it.

4 It is the justice that manifests itself in giving what is due.

Sonnet XI

Injustice, which is falsity and wrong,
is not a part of vice but the whole of it:
where it gains power, every right is dead,
every law, every order, every custom is destroyed;

individual desire becomes its own law.
Woe to a lowly man who is brought before it!
And greater woe to those who profit by it,
and to those, mired in trouble, who hold it above all else!

Justice is all the good one gains from giving
to God, to oneself, and to one's neighbour;
and since it contains every good, it also has every merit.

And every evil is wrong therefore: keeping,
stealing, and giving where one should not; and as
it is pure evil, it surely deserves every evil.

Sonetto XII[1]

O d'onni bono bon, bona vertue,
e ccon cui bon sol bon pote ·se dire;
e bono in sé non-bon, ove non tue,
ni male male, u'· ben può tuo plasire.

Perdita teco tenp' onni pro fue,
e onta onore, e nnoia onni gioire;
pregio, fòr te, e bon omo à dduve?
E bbono teco e ppregio u' pò fallire?

Pover' ricchi, villan' gentil', bassi alti
son teco, e, ffòr te, onni contraro:
gioioze meraviglie in terra fai,

come e sovente [...] rei rubalti.
Tu ssol onore e amor merti charo,
e ssola te Dio ama e pregia assai.

1 Sonnet: ABAB ABAB CDE CDE; v. 7: -uve instead of -ue.

Sonnet XII

Oh good virtue, good of every good,
by which alone good can be called good,
and without which good is not good:
evil is not evil where your pleasure has some power.

With you, every loss is a gain,
every shame an honour, and every trouble a joy.
Without you, where can a man find praise and good?
With you, can good and praise ever be lacking?

The poor are rich, the peasants noble, the low high
with you; without you, quite the contrary.
You make joyous wonders on earth,

when you regularly [...] overthrow evil people.
You alone dearly deserve honour and love,
and God loves and much praises only you.

Sonetto XIII[1]

De vertù de sciensia, il cui podere
e valor grande pò nullo stimare,
merto avant' è; peroché savere
condur vertù vol tucte e allumare.

E dico, poco onni vertù valere
e onni bono, u' ben no sciensia appare.
Vidanda sale e ppan mensa rechere,
ma viapiù vertù sciensa in onni affare.

Sciensia è lluce, cibo e nmedicina,
scudo e spada, che difende e vince:
grandessa, onore fa sovraben tutto.

No è gianmai, seguendo essa, roina;
e onni bon, cho· llei tenendo, vince,
e, sensa lei, di parte onn' è corrotto.

1 Sonnet: ABAB ABAB CDE CDE; v. 14: -otto instead of -utto.

Sonnet XIII

The merit of the virtue of discernment, whose power
and value cannot be overestimated,
stands before all others: knowledge is in fact
necessary to lead and illuminate all virtues.

And every virtue and every good
is of little value where there is no discernment.
Food needs salt and a table needs bread,
but virtue needs discernment even more at all times.

Discernment is light, food, and medicine;
it is a shield and sword that protects and wins;
it makes greatness and honour superior to all other goods.

Discernment will never lead us to ruin:
every good wins by keeping to it,
without it, there can only be suffering.

Sonetto XIV[1]

Tu, costante e ssigur fondamento
de vertù tutta e guardia, umilitate,
fòr cui del tutto vanno in perdimento
perdon, grasi' ed onor, e sson isdegnate;

e in cui prendon pregio e piacimento,
e dda Dio e dda om son meritate.
Teco tenendo, nullo è cchadimento,
ni nmale alcun sor te à podestate.

Tu onni iniqui e rrei vinci de leve,
non sol corpo ma core segon tee;
diavol conquidi e dDio fai che vòi fare.

Al poder tuo non pò poder, né deve;
ben è beato quelli, ove ben se' -e,
e ddove no, mizer del tutto appare.

1 Sonnet: ABAB ABAB CDE CDE.

Sonnet XIV

You constant, safe foundation,
guardian of all virtue, humility,
without which pardon, grace, and honour
are shunned and lost;

and through which they gain praise and pleasure
and are rewarded by God and man.
Holding on to you, one cannot fall,
nor can any evil have power over you.

You easily defeat all those who are guilty and unjust;
they follow you with both body and soul;
you defeat devils, and make God do what you want.

No power can nor should resist your power.
He who has you is blessed
and he who is without you is utterly miserable.

Sonetto XV[1]

Larghessa, tu vertù, dand' e tenendo
ov'è, come, quanto e quando, degnio,
e anche più nemic' -om demettendo,
che sovre onni tu' don mertevil tegnio.

Tu traggi cori con forso a bben voglendo,
e covri, ove se', quazi onni non-degnio.
Omo pentuto assai à, te avendo,
ché tu perdono li· procacci en regnio.[2]

Malvagi, boni, strani ed annemici,
angeli e dDio inn- amor tuo destringi,
se ddegniamente ben retto procedi.

A' ddegni e bizognosi: «È per Dio!», dici;
a rricchi neghi, e rrei fuggi e 'nfingi,
fòr quanto a ggran nicessità li· vedi.

---

1 Sonnet: ABAB ABAB CDE CDE.

2 The kingdom referred to is the eternal one.

Sonnet XV

Generosity, you are a virtue, giving and keeping
where, how, how much, and when it is worthy;
moreover you forgive an enemy his debts,
which is more praiseworthy than all your other gifts.

You forcefully lead hearts to desire good,
and you compensate for almost everything unworthy.
A repentant man has much if he has you,
for you gain him pardon in the kingdom.

Evil people and good ones, foreigners, enemies,
angels, and God are bound by your love,
when you rightfully proceed with dignity.

To the deserving and needy you say: "This is for God,"
to the rich you deny; you shy from the guilty and pretend with them,
except when you see them in great need.

Sonetto XVI[1]

Chastitate, tu luce e ttu bellore
e chandore pregharo inn- onestate,
ismiraldo 'n gienme, roz' èi 'nn- onni fiore,
und' odor è, valor, gran degnitate.

Figlia spesial de dDio, d'angiel' sorore,
tu angielica fai umanitate,
cielestial vivi in terra; a· rre maggiore
tuoi' char' e belle figli' à' isposate.[2]

Reine sono: enpie · si 'l ciel de loro,
sì ccome 'n terra de terrene spose;
e ccelestial spirto è llor dolcessa,

a cui charnal val men che fangho a oro.
Tuoi' gioi sigure, orrate, grasiose,
e dd'onni parte magnia àn' allegressa.

1 Sonnet: ABAB ABAB CDE CDE.
2 These are the nuns, Christ's brides.

Sonnet XVI

Chastity, you have honestly been praised
as light and beauty and candour;
an emerald among gems, you are the rose among flowers,
generating perfume, valour, and great dignity.

Special daughter of God, sister to angels,
you make men seem like angels;
you are celestial yet you live on earth;
you married your dear and beautiful daughters to the highest King.

They are queens: and heaven is full with them,
as earth is with earthly brides;
and their sweetness is celestial spirit,

compared to which carnal sweetness is less than mud is to gold.
Your joys are safe, honourable, gracious,
receiving great happiness from all quarters.

Sonetto XVII[1]

Amistade de 'nvidia è medicina
e de leggero piagha onni sua sana,
ché presioza è ssua vertud' e fina
e bbono è 'l maggio di natura umana.

Luce del mondo e spesial largha vina,
che 'n terra fa-i di bene onni fontana,
pane de vita e de dolsor cocina,
devina grasia en lei giung' e mondana.

E sso' ghaud' è l'autrui come 'l su' bono,
e essa è d'uman ben tutto savore,
in cui bono sa reo e dolse amaro;

vivendo sensa lei, mort' è ciascono,
e ppover tutto lo più ricco signore,
e mizer fort' e vil tutto 'l più charo.

---

1 Sonnet: ABAB ABAB CDE CDE.

Sonnet XVII

Friendship is the medicine for envy
and easily cures all of her wounds,
for its power is precious and refined;
it is the highest good in human nature.

Light of the world, and a singularly rich vein
that nourishes every fountain of good on earth;
bread of life and sweet nourishment;
divine and worldly grace are joined in it.

And its joy is its own good just as it is other people's,
and it is all the flavour of human goodness,
where bad tastes good and bitter sweet.

Without it, no one can live
and the richest lord becomes a poor man,
the strong miserable and what is dearest utterly base.

Sonetto XVIII[1]

Tenperansa di corpo è ssanitade;
vita li· allungha e ghaudio in llui retene,
e ttolle lui dolore e 'nfermitade
e ccure troppo, e ppace in lui convene;

e ppresta sciens' a tenpo e ccharitade,
e ccontr' ogni aversar d'om pugna bene,
e ddà di corpo ad alma podestade,
ed inn- amor di bon lei lo· contene.

Onni vertù in lei pasce e congaude,
e chatuna di lei riceve aiuto.
O!, quanto coronata è bben sua laude!

Tenperat' omo in part' è onni tenuto:
appena più pregiato alcuno s'aude,
ché bon v'è retto e mal nullo 'nvenuto.

1 Sonnet: ABAB ABAB CDC DCD.

Sonnet XVIII

Temperance is health to the body:
it lengthens life and keeps joy within;
it eases pain and sickness
and undue worry and brings peace.

It gives knowledge and charity at the right time,
and fights all foes of man;
it gives the soul lordship over the body
and keeps it loving the good.

Every virtue feeds on it and rejoices in it,
and each accordingly receives help.
Its praise is so duly crowned!

A temperate man is held in esteem everywhere:
one rarely hears of anyone more praised,
for in him is good with no trace of evil.

Sonetto XIX[1]

Pensand' om che val bon dizio, fa d'esso
che dezia. Qual è, no llo· procura?
Non oziozo star mai li· è permesso:
dezio lo· pungie e mette · lo 'n rancura.

Und' a bon dà · n · sse, e, bbon ovrando, spesso
sì fa vertute, quale, se ben dura,
vertuos' e beato om fa appresso,
e ddà bbon tutto: degnio atto e' llavura.

Onni cosa che val, val solamente
da la propia sua operassione;
como non-bono, grand' -omo valente?

Operi bon, chi di bon vol mensione!
E nnon a bon restia già, ma promente
a nmiglior senpre sé pungi' a sperone.

1 Sonnet: ABAB ABAB CDC DCD.

Sonnet XIX

When someone thinks what a good desire is worth, he makes it
what he desires. And who would not go after it?
He is never allowed to be idle:
desire spurs him and torments him.

Thus giving himself to good and doing good, he often
creates such a lasting virtue
that makes man virtuous and blessed afterward,
and gives every goodness. What a worthy act to perform!

Everything of value is only valuable
when used appropriately:
How could an evil man be great and valiant?

He who wants a good reputation should do good!
And he should not stop at the good, but continue
always to do better, spurring himself onward.

Sonetto XX[1]

Dolse vertù, mansuetudo, e ddegnia,
amantissim' a tutti e grasiosa,
no ira mai 'n te né scandal regnia,
ma nel mezzo di guerra, 'n pace, ài posa;

ed in terr' ed in cielo gaudi tu' regnia,
e nnon già t'è nemic' alcuna cosa.
Ira, la qual, contrar' a tte s'assegnia,
che ppió che ffera quazi è fferiosa,

te· deletta, te· chere e te· se· 'nchina,
accioché tu li· aituti onne su' ardore;
e dolcissim' a lei se' medicina.

O!, quanto è bbono tuo, quanto bellore!
Sì ccome naso a vizo è' tu a ddotrina,
tu, di costumi ornament' e colore.

1 Sonnet: ABAB ABAB CDC DCD.

Sonnet XX

Meekness, you are a sweet, dignified virtue,
loving and gracious to all,
no wrath nor scandal ever reigns in you;
you dwell in peace in the midst of war;

You enjoy your reign on earth and in heaven,
and you have no enemies.
Wrath, directing itself towards you,
with nearly as much ferocity as a wild beast,

delights you, needs you, and bows to you
since you may quench its every ardour;
you are a sweet medicine to wrath.

Oh! So great are your goodness and beauty!
You are to doctrine as the nose is to the face,
you add ornament and colour to manners.

Sonetto XXI[1]

O tu, devino amor bon, charitate,
raina de raine e bbon dei boni,
fòr cui giustisia parva à bonitate,
ni vertù val, néd è merto, u' no ·l poni;

giustisia umana, u' tu ài podestate,
no à mister, ché tu sopr' essa doni;
chi à tte, à di bon tutta ubertate,
e cquale no, aver nulla ragioni.

Chatun fòr te inferm' u morto giace,
e in te sana e ven salvo catono,
angeli e hom con Dio ghaldendo in pace.

Sensa te, dico cielo esser non-bono,
e tterra paradizo in te si· face;
e ddov'è', bon per te fatt' è e ver dono.

1 Sonnet: ABAB ABAB CDC DCD.

Sonnet XXI

Oh Charity, you good divine love,
queen of queens and good of goods
without which justice has but little goodness,
and virtue no value; there is no merit where you do not put it.

Where you have lordship, human justice
is unnecessary, for you give much more than it does;
he who has you is rich in goodness;
he who does not, should realize he has nothing.

Without you everybody lies ill or dying,
with you everybody is healed and saved;
angels and man rejoice in peace with God.

Without you, even heaven is not good,
and with you, earth becomes a paradise;
where you are, good is a true gift made by you.

Sonetto XXII[1]

Gloria vera e onor tutto orrato
è render Lui onor, cui solo bono;
in hom per sé no è che mal trovato,
cui no onor, ma onta è guiderdono;

ed altrui bon laudar laid' è peccato,
e nnel secul ontozo esser ragiono.
Fogghа onor, chi vol d'onor gran stato,
e ssegua Dio, cui sol d'onor è dono.

Ché ppicciol Suo vero bon servidore
è, morto, orrato mèi' di vivo ree,
e passa el ciel sua laude e ad angel monta,

e dDio coron' a lui pone d'onore.
Ai!, che mattessa onor tal cangiar è
in vil mondan, ch'è fine etternal onta!

1 Sonnet: ABAB ABAB CDE CDE.

Sonnet XXII

To honour Him, in whom there is only good,
is the true glory and the highest honour.
In man himself there is nothing but evil,
for whom not honour but shame is reward.

Praising other forms of good is an ugly sin,
as, I believe, is living in the shameful world.
He who wants the badge of honour should flee honour,
and follow God, for whom honour is the only gift of honour.

A humble, yet true and good servant of His
is honoured more in death than a living king,
for his praise goes beyond heaven and rises to the angels,

and God gives him a crown of honour.
Ah! What madness it is to exchange such honour
for vain worldly honour, whose end is eternal shame.

Sonetto XXIII[1]

D'animo tu bona vertù, fortessa,
chi degno ben laudar pò tuo valore?
Non pió soavità pregi d'aspressa,
né ttemi povertà pió che riccore.

Non mai visio seguire è tte dolcessa,
ni vertù forte è ben portar dolore;
in morte, s'è mister, prendi vaghessa,
né cosa, mai che visio, ài ·n timore.

Tu pilastro de Giobbo e di Tubia,
tu d'amatori scudo, und'è vittora,
ché non pió re che grilli in timor ài.

Paciensa, costansa e bbaronia
senpre per te in cor d'om se· lavora,
e llaido quanto senti, in lui desfai.

1 Sonnet: ABAB ABAB CDE CDE.

Sonnet XXIII

Fortitude, you good virtue of the soul,
who can rightly praise your worth?
You do not value pleasantness more than hardship,
nor do you fear poverty more than richness.

Following vice is never sweetness to you,
nor is it a great virtue to bear pain;
you take a liking to death when it is necessary,
and you fear nothing but vice.

You are a pillar to Job and Tobias,
a shield to lovers whence victory comes,
for you fear kings no more than crickets.

Through you patience, constancy, and lordship
are always instilled in the heart of man,
where you destroy anything ugly you may find.

Sonetto XXIV[1]

O tu, giustisia, d'onestà sprendore,
non parte de vertù, ma vertù tutta,
in te vertù e bon tutto tuttore,
nel tuo contraro onni malisia addutta.

Non bon ne' rei, fòr te, viver pò fiore:
poder, corp' e spirito in tuo ben frutta;
raina de vertù, tu, non timore
di cos' ài, né dde Dio, bene condutta;

ch'a dDio, ad omo e a catuna cosa
rendi che ddéi in tenpo e in ragione,
ché dirittura è tte sol amorosa.

De' debili tu retta e tu canpione,
in cui fortessa onni lor pace posa,
tu freno a fforti e ttu sor lor bastone.[2]

---

1 Sonnet: ABAB ABAB CDC DCD.

2 The strong are portrayed by the image of untamed horses.

Sonnet XXIV

Oh Justice, you are honesty's splendour,
not a part of virtue but all virtue:
you are always full of virtue and goodness;
while your opposite gathers every malice.

Without you no good person can dwell among evil people;
power, body, and spirit bear fruit because of you;
queen of virtue, when well conducted, you fear
nothing, not even God,

for you give back to God and man and everything
that which you owe in time and quantity,
for righteousness is your only lover.

You support and champion the weak,
in your fortress they find peace,
you are the reins to the strong and the crop that hovers over them.

Sonetto XXV[1]

Charissimi, pió fiate e or appare
ch'è visio, ch'è vertù in part' alcona,
per che se stesso pò matto trovare
chi vertù scifa e bon visio ragiona.

Dio mercé, non déa bon core amare
per se stesso vertù in quanto bona,
e simel visio in lui medesmo odiare?
Quanto viapió per quel che ciascun dona?

O miracol dogliozo e dispiagente:
visio obedir a ddanno, ad onta, a morte;
vertù fugir a vita, a prode e priso,

edd-e a Inferno cheder maggiormente
Zattanàs seguir con pena forte,
che con gioi Dio, bon padre, a pParadiso!

1 Sonnet: ABAB ABAB CDE CDE.

Sonnet XXV

My dearest ones, it is now clear
what vice, and to some degree virtue, is,
so one is surely mad
if he now disdains virtue and deems vice good.

With God's help, should not a good heart love
virtue for its own sake, since it is good,
and similarly hate vice in itself?
And how much more for what each brings?

Oh what a sorrowful and unpleasant miracle:
obeying vice to one's own detriment, shame, and death;
fleeing virtue, from life, valour, and renown,

even asking to follow Satan into hell
with great pain,
rather than with joy, God, the good father, in Paradise!

Sonetto XXVI[1]

Tanto in vertù, frati, de dignitate,
e ssì a rrassional natura avene,
e tanto in visio de malignitate,
e ssì de parte tutte i · desconvene,

che pió val onta e noia e dannitate
con vertù, che con visio onor e bene:
Inferno-a-vertù suavitate
serebbe e Paradizo-a visio pene.

No aspra mai vertù naturalmente,
né visio dolce già, se nnon chadesse
È' u', ragion in natura, e giusto errasse.

Chi fu unque prode-hom, vero valente,
non vita, primaché vertù, perdesse,
e non pió morte che peccato amasse?

1 Sonnet: ABAB ABAB CDE CDE.

Sonnet XXVI

Brothers, there is so much dignity in virtue,
and it must be so according to rational nature;
and there is so much evil in vice,
and so it is inconvenient from every point of view,

that shame, trouble, and harm are worthier
when coupled with virtue, than honour and good are with vice;
Hell would be sweetness to virtue
and Paradise pain to vice.

By nature, virtue is never bitter,
nor is vice ever sweet, unless it occurs
where natural reason and right go wrong.

Was there ever a truly valiant and courageous man
who would not lose his life before his virtue,
and who would not love death rather than sin?

Sonetto XXVII[1]

De visî tutti, frati, e vertù dire
longha fora la tela e anoiosa,
e di ciò, che ditto è, credo venire
onni de visio e de vertude cosa.

Per che chi vuol da visio onni partire
e vertute tener lui delettosa,
entendo ben ch'e' cciò possa fornire,
se ffede retta in isperansa posa.

E anco vol saver certo ciascono,
che non vertù può dir se non vogloza,
o, se per onor, move in mert' alcono:

libera vogla vole e cher ascoza
fare volonter, com' ante un gran comono,
e, in Dio grasia e ssua, star grasioza.

1 Sonnet: ABAB ABAB CDC DCD.

Sonnet XXVII

Brothers, to tell of all vices and virtues
would be a long and tedious story,
and I believe that everything about vice and virtue
follows from what I have said.

Therefore he who wants to abandon all vices
and keep virtue delectable to himself,
can most certainly do it, I see,
if his right faith relies on hope.

Everyone must also know that virtue
cannot be called such unless it is voluntary,
or, if it is performed for honour, it must be directed to something
worthwhile:

free will wishes to act
in secret as ardently as before a great crowd,
and it wishes to keep God's grace and its own.

Bibliography

Texts by Guittone d'Arezzo

Poems (complete editions)

Guittone d'Arezzo. *Rime di fra Guittone d'Arezzo.* Ed. L. Valeriani. 2 vols. Florence: Morandi, 1828.

– *Le rime di Guittone d'Arezzo.* Ed. F. Egidi. Bari: Laterza, 1940.

Poems (partial editions)

Guittone d'Arezzo. *Canzoniere: I sonetti d'amore del codice Laurenziano.* Ed. L. Leonardi. Turin: Einaudi, 1994.

– *Del carnale amore.* Ed. R. Capelli. Rome: Carocci, 2007.

– *Le Rime di Fra Guittone d'Arezzo: Volume primo (versi d'amore).* Ed. F. Pellegrini. Collezione di opere inedite o rare 87. Bologna: Romagnoli Dall'Acqua, 1901.

Letters

Guittone d'Arezzo. *Lettere.* Ed. C. Margueron. Collezione di opere inedite o rare 145. Bologna: Commissione per i testi di lingua, 1990.

– *Le lettere di Frate Guittone d'Arezzo.* Ed. F. Meriano. Bologna: Regia commissione pei testi di lingua, 1922.

Texts by other medieval authors and anthologies of texts

Aimeric de Peguilhan. *The Poems of Aimeric de Peguilhan.* Ed. W.P. Shepard and F.M. Chambers. Evanston, IL: Northwestern University Press, 1950.

Andrea Cappellano. *Trattato d'amore. Andreae Capellani regii francorum* De amore *libri tres. Testo latino con due traduzioni toscane inedite del sec. XIV.* Ed. S. Battaglia. Rome: Perella, 1947.

Antonelli, Roberto, Costanzo Di Girolamo, and Rosario Coluccia, eds. *I poeti della Scuola siciliana.* 3 vols. Milan: Mondadori, 2008.

Arnaut Daniel. *Le canzoni di Arnaut Daniel.* Ed. M. Perugi. Milan-Naples: Ricciardi, 1978.

Benvenuto da Imola. *Benvenuti de Rambaldis de Imola comentum super Dantis Aldigherij Comoediam.* Ed. J.F. Lacaita. 5 vols. Florence: Lacaita, 1887.

Bernart de Ventadorn. *Seine Lieder mit Einleitung und Glossar.* Ed. C. Appel. Halle: Niemeyer, 1915.

Cadenet. *Der trobador Cadenet.* Ed. C. Appel. Halle: Niemeyer, 1920.

– *Les poésies du troubadour Cadenet.* Ed. J. Zemp. Bern, Frankfurt am Main, and Las Vegas: Peter Lang, 1978.

Cavalcanti, Guido. *Rime. Con le rime di Iacopo Cavalcanti.* Ed. D. De Robertis. Turin: Einaudi, 1986.

– *The Selected Poetry of Guido Cavalcanti.* Ed. S. West. Leicester: Troubador, 2009.

– *The Poetry of Guido Cavalcanti.* Ed. L. Nelson, Jr. New York and London: Garland, 1986.

Contini, Gianfranco, ed. *Poeti del Duecento.* 2 vols. Milan-Naples: Ricciardi, 1960.

Dante Alighieri. *Commedia.* Ed. A. Chiavacci Leonardi. 3 vols. Milan: Mondadori, 1997.

– *La Commedia secondo l'antica vulgata.* Ed. G. Petrocchi. 4 vols. Milan: Mondadori, 1966–7; rev. ed., Florence: Le Lettere, 1994.

– *Dante's De vulgari eloquentia.* Ed. and trans. S. Botterill. Cambridge: Cambridge University Press, 1996.

– *Dante's Lyric Poetry.* Ed. K. Foster and P. Boyde. 2 vols. Oxford: Oxford University Press, 1967.

– *De vulgari eloquentia.* In *Opere minori,* ed. and trans. P.V. Mengaldo, 203–37. Milan-Naples: Ricciardi, 1979.

– *The Divine Comedy of Dante Alighieri.* Ed. R.M. Durling and R. Martinez. New York: Oxford University Press, 1996.

– *Opere: Convivio. Monarchia. Epistole. Egloghe.* Ed. M. Santagata. Milan: Mondadori, 2014.

– *Opere: Rime. Vita nova. De vulgari eloquentia.* Ed. M. Santagata. Milan: Mondadori, 2011.

– *Purgatorio.* Ed. R.M. Durling and R. Martinez. New York: Oxford University Press, 2003.

– *Rime.* Ed. G. Contini. Turin: Einaudi, 1995.

– *Rime.* Ed. D. De Robertis. 3 vols. Florence: Le Lettere, 2002.

– *Vita nova.* Ed. G. Gorni. Turin: Einaudi, 1996.

– *Vita nova.* Ed. and trans. A. Frisardi. Evanston, IL: Northwestern University Press, 2012.

– *Vita nuova*. In *Opere minori*, ed. D. De Robertis. Vol. I, pt I. Milan-Naples: Ricciardi, 1984.

Davanzati, Chiaro. *Rime*. Ed. A. Menichetti. Bologna: Commissione per i testi di lingua, 1965.

De Riquer, Martin, ed. *Los trovadores. Historia literaria y textos*. 3 vols. Barcelona: Planeta, 1975.

Folquet de Marselha. *Folquet de Marselha. Poesie*. Ed. P. Squillacioti. Rome: Carocci, 2003.

– *Le poesie di Folchetto di Marsiglia*. Ed. P. Squillacioti. Pisa: Pacini, 1999.

Giuntina. Sonetti e canzoni di diversi antichi autori toscani. Florence: Giunta, 1527.

Golding, Frederick, ed. *Lyrics of the Troubadours and Trouvères: An Anthology and a History*. Gloucester, MA: Peter Smith, 1983.

Guinizzelli, Guido. *Rime*. Ed. L. Rossi. Turin: Einaudi, 2002.

– *The Poetry of Guido Guinizzelli*. Ed. R. Edwards. New York and London: Garland, 1987.

Horgan, Frances, ed. *The Romance of the Rose*. Oxford: Oxford University Press, 1999.

Jensen, Frede, ed. *The Poetry of the Sicilian School*. New York and London: Garland, 1986.

– *Troubadour Lyrics: A Bilingual Anthology*. New York: Peter Lang Publishing, 1999.

– *Tuscan Poetry of the Duecento: An Anthology*. New York and London: Garland, 1995.

Lentini, Giacomo da. *Poesie*. Ed. R. Antonelli. Rome: Bulzoni, 1979.

Marcabru. *Marcabru. A Critical Edition*. Ed. S. Gaunt, R. Harvey, and L. Paterson. Cambridge: D.S. Brewer, 2000.

Monte Andrea da Fiorenza. *Le rime*. Ed. F.F. Minetti. Florence: Accademia della Crusca, 1979.

Perdigon. *Les chansons de Perdigon*. Ed. H.J. Chaytor. Paris: Champion, 1926.

Petrarca, Francesco. *Canzoniere*. Ed. M. Santagata. Milan: Mondadori, 1997.

– *Triumphi*. Ed. M. Ariani. Milan: Mursia, 1988.

Pillet, Alfred, and Henry Carstens. *Bibliographie der Troubadours* (*BdT*). Halle: Niemeyer, 1933. Reprint: Milan: Ledizioni, 2013.

Rigaut de Barbezilh. *Le canzoni*. Ed. M. Braccini. Florence: Olschki, 1960.

Rogier, Peire. *The Poems of the Troubadour Peire Rogier*. Ed. D.E.T. Nichols. Manchester: Manchester University Press, 1976.

Salinari, Carlo, ed. *La poesia lirica del Duecento*. Turin: UTET, 1951; reprint 1968.

Uc Faidit. *The Donatz Provensals of Uc Faidit*. Ed. J.H. Marshall. London: Oxford University Press, 1969.

Vidal, Peire. *Poesie*. Ed. D.S. Avalle. 2 vols. Milan-Naples: Ricciardi, 1960.

Vidal, Raimon. *The "Razos de trobar" of Raimon Vidal and Associated Texts*. Ed. J.H. Marshall. London: Oxford University Press, 1972.

Vidas. Biographies des troubadours, textes provençaux des XIII et XIV siècles. Ed. J. Boutière and A.H. Shutz. Paris: Nizet, 1964.

References

Alfie, Fabian, *Dante's Tenzone with Forese. The Reprehension of Vice*. Toronto: University of Toronto Press, 2011.

Antonelli, Roberto. "Dal notaro a Guinizzelli." In *Da Guinizzelli a Dante: Nuove prospettive sulla lirica del Duecento*, ed. F. Brugnolo and G. Peron, 107–46. Padua: Il Poligrafo, 2004.

– "Perché un libro(-canzoniere)." In *Critica del testo*, VI 1, 2003. *L'io lirico: Francesco Petrarca. Radiografia dei "Rerum vulgarium fragmenta,"* ed. G. Desideri, A. Landolfi, and S. Marinetti, 1:49–65. Rome: Viella, 2003.

– "Struttura materiale e disegno storiografico del canzoniere Vaticano." In *I canzonieri della lirica italiana delle origini*, ed. L. Leonardi, 4:3–23. Florence: SISMEL-Edizioni del Galluzzo, 2001.

– "Subsistant igitur ignorantie sectatores." In *Guittone d'Arezzo nel settimo centenario della morte: Atti del convegno internazionale di Arezzo*, ed. Michelangelo Picone, 337–49. Florence: Cesati Editore, 1995.

Antonello, Armando. "Un'inedita attestazione duecentesca del sonetto 'Omo falito, plen de van pensieri' di Guittone d'Arezzo." *Strumenti critici* 74 (2007): 11–25.

Asperti, Stefano. *Carlo I d'Angiò e i trovatori.* Ravenna: Longo, 1995.

Avalle, D'Arco Silvio. *Ai luoghi di delizia pieni.* Milan-Naples: Ricciardi, 1977.

– *I manoscritti della letteratura in lingua d'oc*. Ed. L. Leonardi. Turin: Einaudi, 1993.

– "Un 'vanto' di Guittone." *Cultura neolatina* 37 (1977): 161–6.

– ed. *Concordanze della lingua poetica italiana delle origini* (*CLPIO*). Milan-Naples: Ricciardi, 1992.

Baehr, R. "Studien zur Rhetorik in den Reimen Guittones von Arezzo." *Zeitschrift für romanische Philologie* 73 (1957): 193–258, 357–415; 74 (1958): 163–211.

Baranski, Zygmunt G. "''nfiata labbia' and 'dolce stil novo': A Note on Dante, Ethics, and the Technical Vocabulary of Literature." In *Sotto il segno di Dante. Scritti in onore di Francesco Mazzoni*, ed. L. Coglievina and D. De Robertis, 17–35. Florence: Le Lettere, 1998.

Barillari, Sonia Maura, ed. *Dalla Provenza al Monferrato. Percorsi medievali di testi e musiche.* Alessandria: Edizioni dell'Orso, 2007.

Barolini, Teodolinda. *Dante and the Origins of Italian Literary Culture*. New York: Fordham University Press, 2006.

– *Dante's Poets: Textuality and Truth in the "Comedy."* Princeton, NJ: Princeton University Press, 1984.

Beltrami, Pietro. *Metrica italiana*. Bologna: Il Mulino, 1991.

– "Spigolature su Sordello e la poesia italiana del Duecento." In *Sordello da Goito. Atti del convegno (Goito Mantova, 13–15 1997) Cultura neolatina* 60, n. 3–4 (2000): 233–79.

Bertini, Ferruccio. "Equivoci e doppi sensi nel *De* amore di Andrea Cappellano." In *Studi sul* De amore *di Andrea Cappellano e sulla sua posterità volgare*, ed. Margherita Lecco, 37–56. Alessandria: Edizioni dell'Orso, 2006. [*Immagine Riflessa* N.S. Anno XV (2006) N. 2 (Luglio-Dicembre)].

Bertolucci Pizzorusso, Valeria. *Morfologie del testo medievale*. Bologna: Il Mulino, 1989.

Bettarini, Rosanna. "Croci e delizie." In *Operosa Parva per Gianni Antonini*, ed. D. De Robertis and F. Gavazzeni, 25–32. Verona: Valdonega, 1996.

Bianco, Monica. "Quarantena guittoniana in un autografo di Domenico Venier." *Medioevo romanzo* 32 (2008): 85–115.

Boitani, Piero. "'Ridon le carte.' Guerra e pace nella tradizione." *Strumenti critici* 25 (2010): 3–10.

Bologna, Corrado. "L'esperimento di Guittone." In *Storia della letteratura italiana Salerno*, 1:420–34. Rome: Salerno, 1995.

– *Tradizione e fortuna dei classici italiani. Dalle origini al Tasso*. Turin: Einaudi, 1994.

Borra, Antonello. "Guittone all'Inferno?" *Italica* 93 (2016): 23–36.

– "Guittone D'Arezzo." *Encyclopedia of Italian Literary Studies*, 925–8. New York and London: Routledge, 2007.

– *Guittone d'Arezzo e le maschere del poeta: La lirica cortese tra ironia e palinodia*. Ravenna: Longo editore, 2000.

Borsa, Paolo. *La nuova poesia di Guido Guinizzelli*. Fiesole (Florence): Cadmo, 2007.

– "La tenzone tra Guido Guinizzelli e frate Guittone d'Arezzo." *Studi e problemi di critica testuale* 65 (2002): 47–88.

– "Tra etica e retorica. Il motivo della lode 'in faccia' da Guittone a Dante." In *Per Franco Brioschi. Saggi di lingua e letteratura italiana*, 23–35. Milan: Cisalpino, 2007.

Bowden, Betsy. "The Art of Courtly Copulation." *Mediaevalia et Humanistica* 9 (1979): 67–85.

Brugnolo, Furio. "La scuola poetica siciliana." In *Storia della letteratura italiana Salerno*, ed. E. Malato, 1:265–337. Rome: Salerno, 2001.

Bruni, Francesco. "Agonismo guittoniano. Risemantizzazione, polisemia e colori dell'ambiguità in una sequenza di sonetti." In *Guittone d'Arezzo nel settimo centenario della morte: Atti del convegno internazionale di Arezzo*, ed. Michelangelo Picone, 89–123. Florence: Cesati Editore, 1995.

– "Critica della cortesia e poesia etico-religiosa: Il nuovo Guittone." In *Storia della civiltà letteraria italiana*, 1:310–17. Turin: UTET, 1990.

– "Le parole e i fatti: L'ambiguità di amore secondo Guittone." In *Storia della civiltà letteraria italiana*, 1:295–306. Turin: UTET, 1990.

Calenda, Corrado. *Appartenenze metriche ed esegesi. Dante, Cavalcanti, Guittone.* Naples: Bibliopolis, 1995.

– "I Siculo-toscani." In *Manuale di letteratura italiana*, ed. F. Brioschi and C. Di Girolamo, 1:311–24. Turin: Bollati-Boringhieri, 1993.

Capelli, Roberta. "'Amor si pinge figurato'? Guittone (non) risponde." *Italianistica* 39 (2009): 11–19.

Carpi, Umberto. *La nobiltà di Dante.* Florence: Edizioni Polistampa, 2004.

Carrai, Stefano. *La lirica toscana del Duecento. Cortesi, guittoniani, stilnovisti.* Rome and Bari: Laterza, 1997.

Cella, Roberta. *I gallicismi nei testi dell'italiano antico (dalle origini alla fine del sec. XIV).* Florence: Accademia della Crusca, 2003.

Cherchi, Paolo. *Andreas and the Ambiguity of Courtly Love.* Toronto: University of Toronto Press, 1994.

– "L'epifrasi in Guittone." In *Guittone d'Arezzo nel settimo centenario della morte: Atti del convegno internazionale di Arezzo*, ed. Michelangelo Picone, 33–52. Florence: Cesati Editore, 1995.

Ciccuto, Marcello. "Dante e Bonagiunta. Reperti allusivi nel canto XXIV del *Purgatorio*." *Lettere italiane* 34 (1982): 386–95.

– "Guinizzelli e Guittone, Barberino e Petrarca: Le origini del libro volgare illustrato." *Rivista di storia della miniatura* 1–2 (1996–7): 77–88.

– "Meo e Guittone." *Italianistica* 8 (1979): 3–25.

Coluccia, Rosario, and Riccardo Gualdo, eds. *Dai siciliani ai siculo-toscani. Lingua, metro e stile per la definizione del canone. Atti del convegno (Lecce, 21–23 aprile 1998).* Galatina: Congedo editore, 1999.

Contini, Gianfranco. "Guittone in quarantena." In *Studi medievali in onore di Antonino de Stefano*, 561–7. Palermo: Società Italiana di Storia Patria, 1956.

– *Un'idea di Dante: Saggi danteschi.* Turin: Einaudi, 1976.

– Review of Francesco Egidi, *Le rime di Guittone d'Arezzo. Giornale storico della letteratura italiana* 117 (1941): 55–82.

Debenedetti, Santorre. *Letteratura italiana delle origini.* Florence: Sansoni, 1970.

– *Nuovi studi sulla Giuntina di rime antiche.* Ed. Cesare Segre. Turin: Aragno, 2011.

De Laude, Silvia. "La lingua madre della poesia." In *Atlante della letteratura italiana*, ed. Sergio Luzzatto and Gabriele Pedullà, 1:18–26. Turin: Einaudi, 2010.

Del Monte, Alberto. "Guittone dell'aridità." In *Studi sulla poesia ermetica medievale*, 113–38. Naples: Giannini, 1953.

De Lollis, Cesare. "Arnaldo e Guittone." In *Scrittori d'Italia*, ed. G. Contini and V. Santoli, 3–19. Milan-Naples: Ricciardi, 1968.

Del Sal, Nevio. "Guittone (e i guittoniani) nella *Commedia*." *Studi danteschi* 61 (1989): 109–52.

De Sanctis, Francesco. *Storia della letteratura italiana*. Ed. G. Contini. Turin: UTET, 1973.

Di Girolamo, Costanzo. *Trovatori*. Turin: Bollati Boringhieri, 1989.

Durling, Robert M. "Mio figlio ov'è? (*Inferno* X, 60)." In *Dante. Da Firenze all'aldilà*, ed. Michelangelo Picone, 303–29. Florence: Cesati, 2001.

Egidi, Francesco. "Un trattato d'Amore inedito di Guittone." *Giornale storico della letteratura italiana* 97 (1931): 49–70.

Ferroni, Giulio, Andrea Cortellessa, Italo Pantani, and Silvia Tatti. *Storia e testi della letteratura italiana. Dalle origini al 1300*. Milan: Mondadori, 2002.

Folena, Gianfranco. "Pensamento guittoniano." *Lingua nostra* 16 (1955): 100–4.

– "Überlieferungsgeschichte der altitalienischen Literatur." In *Geschichte der Textüberlieferung der antiken und mittelalterlichen Literatur*, ed. H. Hunger, 2:319–537. Zürich: Atlantis Verlag, 1964.

Formentin, Vittorio. *Poesia italiana delle origini. Storia linguistica italiana*. Rome: Carocci, 2007.

Frank, István. *Répertoire métrique de la poésie des troubadours*. 2 vols. Paris: Champion, 1966.

Fratta, Aniello. *Le fonti provenzali dei poeti della scuola siciliana*. Florence: Le Lettere, 1996.

Gaspary, Adolf. *La scuola poetica siciliana del secolo XIII*. Livorno: Vigo, 1882.

Giorgi, Rossana. "Analisi linguistica del Canzoniere Palatino." In *Concordanze della lingua poetica italiana delle origini* (*CLPIO*), ed. D'Arco Silvio Avalle, clxi–clxvi. Milan-Naples: Ricciardi, 1992.

Giunta, Claudio. *Codici. Saggi sulla poesia del medioevo*. Bologna: Il Mulino, 2005.

– *Due saggi sulla tenzone*. Padua: Antenore, 2002.

– "Un'ipotesi sulla morfologia del canzoniere Vaticano lat. 3793." *Studi di filologia italiana* 53 (1995): 23–54.

– *La poesia italiana nell'età di Dante. La linea Bonagiunta-Guinizzelli*. Bologna: Il Mulino, 1998.

– "Poesie che commentano poesie nel Medioevo. Il caso di Guittone d'Arezzo." In *L'autocommento: Atti della giornata di studi*, 1–22. Alessandria: Edizioni dell'Orso, 2004.

Gorni, Guglielmo. *Dante prima della "Commedia."* Fiesole: Cadmo, 2001.

– "Guittone e Dante," in *Guittone d'Arezzo nel settimo centenario della morte: Atti del convegno internazionale di Arezzo*, ed. Michelangelo Picone, 309–35. Florence: Cesati Editore, 1995.

– "Il nodo della lingua." In *Il nodo della lingua e il verbo d'amore. Studi su Dante e altri duecentisti*, 13–21. Florence: Olschki, 1981.

Holmes, Olivia. *Assembling the Lyric Self: Authorship from Troubadour Song to Italian Poetry Book.* Minneapolis: University of Minnesota Press, 2000.

Honess, Claire. "Dante and Political Poetry in the Vernacular." *Journal of the Institute of Romance Studies*, 6 (1998), 21–42; also in *Dante and his Literary Precursors*, ed. J.C. Barnes and J. Petrie, 117–51. Dublin: Four Courts Press, 2007.

Kay, Tristan. *Dante's Lyric Redemption. Eros, Salvation, Vernacular Tradition.* Oxford: Oxford University Press, 2016.

– "Redefining the 'matera amorosa': Dante's *Vita nova* and Guittone's (Anti-) courtly *Canzoniere.*" *Italianist* 29 (2009): 369–99.

Keen, Catherine. "'Va, mia canzone': Textual Transmission and the Congedo in Medieval Exile Lyrics." *Italian Studies* 64 (2009): 183–97.

Lazzerini, Lucia. *Letteratura medievale in lingua d'oc.* Modena: Mucchi Editore, 2001.

Lecco, Margherita, ed. *Studi sul* De amore *di Andrea Cappellano e sulla sua posterità volgare.* Alessandria: Edizioni dell'Orso, 2006.

Le Lay, Cécile. "Une lettre pour 'rétracter' après la 'Chanson de Montaperti'?" *Arzanà* 12 (2007): 17–36.

Leonardi, Lino. "Appunti su Guittone nei *Rerum vulgarium fragmenta.*" *Critica del testo* 6 (2003): 353–66.

– "Guittone cortese?" *Medioevo romanzo* 13 (1988): 421–55.

– "Guittone e dintorni. Arezzo, lo 'Studium' e la prima rivoluzione della poesia italiana." In *750 anni degli statuti universitari aretini. Atti del convegno internazionale su origini, maestri, discipline e ruolo culturale dello Studium di Arezzo, Arezzo, 16–18 febbraio 2005*, ed. F. Stella, 205–23. Florence: SISMEL-Edizioni del Galluzzo, 2006.

– "La poesia delle origini e del Duecento." In *Storia della letteratura Italiana Salerno*, ed. E. Malato, 10:5–89. Rome: Salerno, 2001.

– "Tradizione e ironia nel primo Guittone." In *Guittone d'Arezzo nel settimo centenario della morte: Atti del convegno internazionale di Arezzo*, ed. Michelangelo Picone, 138–48. Florence: Cesati Editore, 1995.

– ed. *I canzonieri della lirica italiana della origini.* 4 vols. Florence: SISMEL-Edizioni del Galluzzo, 2000–1.

– ed. *Il canzoniere Riccardiano di Guittone*. Florence: SISMEL-Edizioni del Galluzzo, 2010.

Leporatti, Roberto. "Il 'libro' di Guittone e la *Vita nova*." *Nuova rivista di letteratura italiana* 4 (2001): 41–150.

Marchesani, Andrea. Review of Roberta Capelli, *Del carnale amore. Rassegna della letteratura italiana* 112 (2008): 168–71.

Margueron, Claude. *Recherches sur Guittone d'Arezzo, sa vie, son époque, sa culture*. Paris: Presses Universitaires de France, 1966.

Marti, Mario. *Ultimi contributi dal certo al vero*. Galatina: Congedo, 1995.

Mazzotta, Giuseppe. *Dante, Poet of the Desert: History and Allegory in the Divine Comedy*. Princeton,NJ: Princeton University Press, 1979.

Meneghetti, Maria Luisa. *Il pubblico dei trovatori*. Turin: Einaudi, 1992.

Millspaugh, Scott. "'Trobar clus' in the Early Italian Lyric: Textual Enclosure, Social Space, and the Poetry of Guittone d'Arezzo." *Italian Studies* 68 (2013): 1–16.

Minetti, Francesco Filippo. *Sondaggi guittoniani*. Turin: Giappichelli, 1974.

Moleta, Vincent. *The Early Poetry of Guittone d'Arezzo*. London: The Modern Humanities Research Association, 1976. Trans. *Guittone cortese*. Naples: Liguori, 1987.

Morlino, Luca. "La letteratura francese e provenzale nell'Italia medievale." In *Atlante della letteratura italiana*, ed. S. Luzzatto and G. Pedullà, 1:27–40. Turin: Einaudi, 2010.

Orlando, Silvio. "Due ballate di Guittone d'Arezzo." *Rivista di studi testuali* 2 (2000): 163–82.

Panvini, Bruno. "Studio sui manoscritti dell'antica lirica italiana." *Studi di filologia italiana* 11 (1953): 5–135.

Parducci, A. "La lettera d'amore nell'antica letteratura provenzale." *Studi Medievali* 15 (1942): 69–110.

Parodi, Ernesto Giacomo. *Lingua e letteratura. Studi di teoria linguistica e di storia dell'italiano antico*. Ed. G. Folena. Venice: Neri Pozza, 1957.

Pasero, Nicolò. "Contributi all'interpretazione del sonetto." *Medioevo letterario d'Italia* 6 (2009): 25–43.

Pelaez, Mario. Review of Francesco Pellegrini, *Le Rime di Fra Guittone d'Arezzo: Volume primo (versi d'amore)*. *Giornale storico della letteratura italiana* 41 (1902): 354–64.

Pellizzari, Achille. *La vita e le opere di Guittone d'Arezzo*. Pisa: Nistri, 1906.

Pertile, Lino. "L'altro viaggio di Dante." *Dante* 4 (2008): 25–30.

– "Il nodo di Bonagiunta, le penne di Dante e il Dolce Stil Novo." *Lettere italiane* 46 (1994): 44–75.

Picone, Michelangelo. "Filologia cinquecentesca: I Giunti editori di Guittone." *Yearbook of Italian Studies* 2 (1972): 78–101.
– "Guittone, Guinizzelli e Dante." *L'Alighieri* 42 (2001): 5–19.
– "Lettura guittoniana: La canzone *Ora che la freddore*." *Yearbook of Italian Studies* 5 (1983): 102–16.
– *Percorsi della lirica duecentesca*. Florence: Cadmo, 2003.
– ed. *Guittone d'Arezzo nel settimo centenario della morte: Atti del convegno internazionale di Arezzo*. Florence: Cesati Editore, 1995.
Pittaluga, Stefano. "Andrea Cappellano e la letteratura d'amore del XII secolo." In *Studi sul* De amore *di Andrea Cappellano e sulla sua posterità volgare*, ed. Margherita Lecco, 117–27. Alessandria: Edizioni dell'Orso, 2006. [*Immagine Riflessa* N.S. Anno XV (2006) N. 2 (Luglio-Dicembre)].
Poli, Andrea. "Una scheda provenzale per Guittone. Le canzoni XX, 'Ahi lasso, che li boni e li malvagi,' e XLIX, 'Altra fiata aggio già, donne, parlato.'" *Filologia e critica* (2000): 95–108.
Pollidori, Valentina. "Appunti sulla lingua del canzoniere Palatino." In *I canzonieri della lirica italiana delle origini. Studi critici*, ed. Lino Leonardi, 4:351–91. Florence: SISMEL-Edizioni del Galluzzo, 2001.
Pötters, Wilhelm. *Nascita del sonetto. Metrica e matematica al tempo di Federico II*. Ravenna: Longo, 1998.
Praloran, Marco. "Alcune osservazioni sulla storia dell'endecasillabo." In *Testi e linguaggi per Paolo Zolli*, 19–39. Modena: Mucchi, 2001.
Quaglio, Antonio Enzo. "L'esperimento di Guittone d'Arezzo." In *Le origini e la Scuola siciliana*, 259–300. Vol. 1 of *Letteratura italiana Laterza*. Bari: Laterza, 1971.
Rapisarda, Stefano, and Orazio Croce. "Cinque paradigmi per il *De amore*." In *Studi sul* De amore *di Andrea Cappellano e sulla sua posterità volgare*, ed. Margherita Lecco, 129–48. Alessandria: Edizioni dell'Orso, 2006. [*Immagine Riflessa* N.S. Anno XV (2006) N. 2 (Luglio-Dicembre)].
Rea, Roberto. "Guinizzelli 'praised and explained.'" *Italianist* 30 (2010): 1–17.
Robertson, Durant Waite, Jr. "The Subject of the *De Amore* of Andreas Capellanus." *Modern Philology* 50 (1952–3): 145–61.
Robin, Anne. "Exercices de style pour hypothèses courtoises: Les chansons 1 et 16 et la lettre V de Guittone d'Arezzo." *Arzanà* 12 (2007): 37–63.
– "Le refus du dialogue: Les sonnets 37–49 de Guittone d'Arezzo." *Arzanà* 9 (2003): 43–64.
Roncaglia, Aurelio. *Le origini della lingua e della letteratura italiana*. Turin: UTET, 2006.
Rossi, Luciano. "Guittone, i trovatori e i trovieri." In *Guittone d'Arezzo nel settimo centenario della morte: Atti del convegno internazionale di Arezzo*, ed. Michelangelo Picone, 11–31. Florence: Cesati Editore, 1995.

Santagata, Mario. *Dal sonetto al canzoniere.* Padua: Liviana, 1979.

Savino, Giancarlo. "Il canzoniere Palatino: Una raccolta 'disordinata'?" In *I canzonieri della lirica italiana delle origini*, ed. Lino Leonardi, 4:301–15. Florence: SISMEL-Edizioni del Galluzzo, 2001.

Segre, Cesare. *Lingua, stile e società.* Milan: Feltrinelli, 1991.

– "Per Guittone." *Studi di filologia italiana* 20 (1962): 5–11.

Segre, Cesare, and Mario Marti, eds. *La prosa del Duecento.* Milan-Naples: Ricciardi, 1959.

Solimena, Adriana. *Repertorio metrico dei poeti siculo-toscani.* Palermo: Centro di studi filologici e linguistici siciliani, 2000.

Steinberg, Justin. *Accounting for Dante. Urban Readers and Writers in Late Medieval Italy.* Notre Dame, IN: University of Notre Dame Press, 2007.

Storey, H. Wayne. "Sulle orme di Guittone: I programmi grafico-visivi del codice Banco Rari 217." In *Studi vari di lingua e letteratura italiana in onore di Giuseppe Velli*, 1:93–105. 2 vols. Milan: Cisalpino, 2002.

Suitner, Franco. "La poesia medievale dedicata alla Madonna: Qualche aspetto tematico." *Rivista di letteratura italiana* 25 (2007): 9–24.

Surdich, Luigi. Review of Cécile Le Lay, "Une lettre pour 'rétracter' après la 'Chanson de Montaperti'?" *Rassegna della letteratura italiana* 112 (2008): 164–5.

Tartaro, Achille. *Il manifesto di Guittone e altri studi fra Due e Quattrocento.* Rome: Bulzoni, 1974.

Terrusi, Leonardo. "Guittone, la 'triaca' e il 'veneno.' Per la storia di un antico tema letterario." In *Studi in onore di Michele Dell'Aquila.* Bari: La nuova ricerca, 2002.

Torraca, Francesco. *Studi di storia letteraria.* Florence: Sansoni, 1923.

Vecchi Galli, Paola. "Onomastica petrarchesca. Per il *Canzoniere.*" *Italique. Poesie Italienne de la Renaissance* 8 (2005): 27–44.

Vilella, Eduard. "Hermetismo y aridità en Guittone." In *Lengua y lenguaje poetico. Actas de IX Congreso Nacional de Italianistas. Universidad de Valladolid (2–4 octubre de 2000)*, ed. S. Porras Castro. Valladolid: Universidad de Valladolid, 2001.

Index of Names

www.ingramcontent.com/pod-product-compliance
Lightning Source LLC
LaVergne TN
LVHW090156080826
844660LV00013B/833/J